14 Days Prayer To Overcome Stubborn Situations

TIMOTHY ATUNNISE

TSA SOLUTION PUBLISHING
ATLANTA, GEORGIA

OVERCOME STUBBORN SITUATION

Copyright © 2016 by Timothy Atunnise

All rights reserved. No part of this book may be reproduced, copied, stored or transmitted in any form or by any means – graphic, electronic, or mechanical, including photocopying, recording, or information storage and retrieval systems without the prior written permission of TSA Solution Publishing except where permitted by law.

Unless otherwise specified, all Scripture quotations in this book are from The Holy Bible, King James Version. KJV is Public domain in the United States printed in 1987.

GLOVIM PUBLICATIONS
1078 Citizens Pkwy
Suite A
Morrow, Georgia 30260
glovimbooks@gmail.com
www.glovimonline.org

TSA Solution Publishing
A division of Timat Store, LLC.
Atlanta, GA 30294
timatstore@yahoo.com

Cover Design: Tim Atunnise

Printed in the United States of America

IMPORTANT NOTICE

Deliverance is a benefit of the Kingdom, only for the children of God. If you have not accepted Jesus Christ as your personal Lord and Savior, this is the best time to do so.

Before you continue, you need to be sure you are in the right standing with God if you want to exercise authority and power in the name of Jesus Christ. The Bible says,
"Then he called his twelve disciples together, and gave them power and authority over all devils, and to cure diseases." - Luke 9:1

"And these signs shall follow them that believe; in my name shall they cast out devils; they shall speak with new tongues; they shall take up serpents; and if they drink any deadly thing, it shall not hurt them; they shall lay hands on the sick, and they shall recover." – Mark 16:17-18.

These are promises for the Children of God, not just for everyone. Why don't you give your life to Christ today and you will have access to the same promises. Food that is meant for the children will not be given to the dogs.

"But he answered and said, it is not meet to take the children's bread, and cast it to dogs" – Matthew 15:26.

If you really want to be delivered from any bondage of the wicked and be set free from any form of captivity, I ask you today to give your life to Christ. If you are ready, say this prayer with all your heart:

"Dear Heavenly Father, You have called me to Yourself in the name of Your dear Son Jesus Christ. I realize that Jesus Christ is the only Way, the Truth, and the Life.

I acknowledge to You that I am a sinner. I believe that Your only begotten Son Jesus Christ shed His precious blood on the cross, died for my sins, and rose again on the third day. I am truly sorry for the deeds which I have committed against You, and therefore, I am willing to repent (turn away from my sins). Have mercy on me, a sinner. Cleanse me, and forgive me of my sins.

I truly desire to serve You, Lord Jesus. Starting from now, I pray that You would help me to hear Your still small voice. Lord, I desire to be led by Your Holy Spirit so I can faithfully follow You and obey all of Your commandments. I ask You for the strength to love You more than anything else so I won't fall back into my old ways. I also ask You to bring genuine believers into my life who will encourage me to live for You and help me stay accountable.

Jesus, I am truly grateful for Your grace which has led me to repentance and has saved me from my sins. By the indwelling of Your Holy Spirit, I now have the power to overcome all sin which before so easily entangled me. Lord Jesus, please transform my life so that I may bring glory and honor to You alone and not to myself.

Right now I confess Jesus Christ as the Lord of my life. With my heart, I believe that God the Father raised His Son Jesus Christ from the dead. This very moment I acknowledge that Jesus Christ is my Savior and according to His Word, right now I am born again. Thank You Jesus, for coming into my life and hearing my prayer. I ask all of this in the name of my Lord and Savior, Jesus Christ. Amen".

I hereby congratulate and welcome you into the Kingdom. You hereby have full access to the benefits, promises and blessings of the Kingdom.

This book is loaded with blessings, you will not be disappointed as you continue to enjoy the goodness of the Lord.

INSTRUCTIONS

If you are new to this method of prayer, please follow this instruction carefully:

Step 1:

Spend enough time in praising and worshiping God not just for what He is about to do or what He has done, but WHO HE IS.

Step 2:

Unforgiveness will surely hinder your prayer, take time to remember all those who have done you wrong, and forgive them from the bottom of your heart. THIS IS VERY IMPORTANT BECAUSE YOUR DELIVERANCE DEPENDS ON IT.

Step 3:

Believe in your heart that God will answer your prayer when you call upon Him, and do not doubt in your heart.

Step 4:

Pray in the name of Jesus Christ alone.

Step 5:

Repeat each prayer point 25 to 30 times or until you are convinced that you receive answer before you go to the next prayer point. Example: When you take prayer point number 1, you say this prayer over and over again, 25 – 30 times or until you are convinced that you have an answer before you go to prayer point number 2.

Step 6:

It will be more effective if you can fast along with your prayer. If you want total deliverance from your bondage, take 3 days of sacrifice in fasting as you say your prayer aggressively, asking your situation to receive permanent solution and YOUR DELIVERANCE WILL BE MADE PERFECT IN THE NAME OF JESUS CHRIST. AMEN!

Table of Contents

Important Notice 4

Instructions 7

Day One 11

Day Two 21

Day Three 31

Day Four 39

Day Five 47

Day Six 55

Day Seven 61

Day Eight 67

Day Nine 75

Day Ten 85

Day Eleven 97

Day Twelve 107

Day Thirteen 115

Day Fourteen 121

But this kind does not go out except by prayer and fasting.
- Matthew 17:21

DAY ONE

RISING ABOVE STUBBORN SITUATION

Passages To Read Before You Pray:
Habakkuk 1:5, Mark 11:22-24, Matthew 16:19, Psalms 9, 18, 30, 55, 86

In the book of Job 22:28, the Scripture says when I decree a thing, it shall be established for me. I stand on this Scripture and decree. I have come into the presence of God today to plead my case. I enter through the gate of praise, into the sanctuary of heaven. I cover myself in the precious blood of Jesus Christ. I baptize myself in the fire of the Holy Ghost. I charge this atmosphere with the fire of God, and I take this neighborhood for the Lord. I arrest every principality and power, territorial spirit, and every throne and kingdom that is not of God. I cast you down and I command you never to lift yourself up against me, because I have the life of God in me.

In the name of Jesus Christ, I confess my sins today, and I ask you O Lord to forgive me on the basis of your mercy. With all my heart, I forgive those who have sinned against me; from the past through this moment. I release them from any form of guilt and shame, in the name of Jesus Christ. I hereby plead the blood of Jesus over any sins committed by my parents and ancestors. I cancel through the Blood of Jesus Christ, any satanic covenants, exchanges, vows or transactions, made over my life, body, soul, spirit, and circumstances, in the name of Jesus Christ. I cancel every legal right that the devil may have against me, by the blood of Jesus Christ. The accuser of the brethren will have nothing against me, as I come to the presence of God in prayer.

The devil cannot hinder or delay my prayer, because I know who I am. I am a child of the Kingdom. I am a king and priest of the Lord, redeemed from the hand of the devil by the blood of Jesus Christ. I walk in power. I walk in miracle. Proverbs 18:21 says, death and life are in the power of my tongue; I command the power in my tongue to manifest now. I command my tongue to become fire, to consume all the powers of darkness in the air, the land, the sea, and beneath the earth. I hereby raise Holy Ghost standard against the prince of the power of the air and all the hosts of darkness in the air. I raise Holy Ghost standard against the queen of the coasts and all the hosts of darkness on the land. I raise Holy Ghost standard against the marine kingdom and all the hosts of darkness in the sea. I raise Holy Ghost standard against the kingdom of hell and all the hosts of darkness beneath the earth. I shoot down all the networks of demons gathering to resist my prayers. I rebuke and bind all the controlling forces of darkness standing against my prayers.

I declare that all satanic thrones, altars, dominions, principalities, powers, rulers of darkness, queens of the coast, queens of heavens, household wickedness, spiritual hosts of wickedness and all satanic works, have no power or authority over my life. I declare that satanic harassment and intimidation have no effect on me.

Today, I receive divine strength to pray; I will not pray in vain. I will not pray amiss. My prayers will bring the desired results. I command the fountain of prayer to open now, and to flow into my life, I command the warring angels of God to descend and fight on my behalf. Every minute and every hour that I spend in prayer, will bring solution. Every prayer point will attract divine attention and divine intervention. I decree open heavens over my

prayers, and today, God of heaven and earth will attend to my case. My prayers today will shake the heavens and move the earth. Testimonies, miracles, healings, breakthroughs, and signs and wonders, will follow my prayers. At the end of this prayer session, my life will never be the same again.

PRAYER POINTS

1. O God my Father, thank you for being my God, my Father and my friend.
2. O God my Father, thank you for the privilege to know you and the power of the resurrection of Jesus Christ.
3. O God my Father, thank you for always being there for me and with me.
4. O God my Father, thank you for the great and mighty things that you are doing in my life.
5. O God my Father, thank you for your provision and protection over me and my household.
6. O God my Father, thank you for always answering my prayers.
7. I confess my sins before you today and I ask you to forgive me on the basis of your mercy, in the name of Jesus Christ.
8. Wash me clean today O Lord by the blood of Jesus Christ.
9. I cover myself and my household with the blood of Jesus Christ.
10. My prayers today will not go in vain; my prayers will produce the desired results in the name of Jesus Christ.
11. I receive the anointing to rise up from every impossible situation. I will not be overwhelmed, in the name of

Jesus Christ.
12. I receive the anointing to rise up from bed of sickness. I will not be overwhelmed, in the name of Jesus Christ.
13. I receive the anointing to rise up from every situation that's challenging my faith. I will not be overwhelmed, in the name of Jesus Christ.
14. I receive the anointing to rise up from every situation that's challenging what God can or cannot do in my life. I will not be overwhelmed, in the name of Jesus Christ.
15. I receive the anointing to rise up from every difficult situation. I will not be overwhelmed, in the name of Jesus Christ.
16. I receive the anointing to rise up from every stubborn situation. I will not be overwhelmed, in the name of Jesus Christ.
17. I receive the anointing to rise up from every turbulent situation. I will not be overwhelmed, in the name of Jesus Christ.
18. I receive the anointing to rise up from every area where I have fallen. I will not be defeated, in the name of Jesus Christ.
19. I receive the anointing to rise up from the state of infirmity. I refuse to give up, in the name of Jesus Christ.
20. I receive the anointing to rise up from the dungeon of poverty. I refuse to give up, in the name of Jesus Christ.
21. I receive the anointing to rise up from the pit of loneliness. I refuse to give up, in the name of Jesus Christ.
22. I receive the anointing to rise up from the pit of trouble. I refuse to give up, in the name of Jesus Christ.
23. I receive the anointing to rise up from the pit of temptation. I refuse to give up, in the name of Jesus

Christ.
24. I receive the anointing to rise up from the pit of trials. I refuse to give up, in the name of Jesus Christ.
25. I receive the anointing to rise up from the pit of financial loss. I refuse to give up, in the name of Jesus Christ.
26. I receive the anointing to rise up from the pit of depression. I refuse to give up, in the name of Jesus Christ.
27. I receive the anointing to rise up from the pit of repression. I refuse to give up, in the name of Jesus Christ.
28. I receive the anointing to rise up from the pit of oppression. I refuse to give up, in the name of Jesus Christ.
29. I receive the anointing to rise up from the pit of affliction. I refuse to give up, in the name of Jesus Christ.
30. I receive the anointing to rise up from the pit of employment struggles. I refuse to give up, in the name of Jesus Christ.
31. I receive the anointing to rise up from the pit of evil cycles. I refuse to give up, in the name of Jesus Christ.
32. I receive the anointing to rise up from the pit of pain. I refuse to give up, in the name of Jesus Christ.
33. I receive the anointing to rise up from the pit of self-inflicted problems. I refuse to give up, in the name of Jesus Christ.
34. I receive the anointing to rise up from the pit of demotion. I refuse to give up, in the name of Jesus Christ.
35. I receive the anointing to rise up from the prison of self-pity. I refuse to give up, in the name of Jesus Christ.

36. I receive the anointing to rise up from the prison of slow progress. I refuse to give up, in the name of Jesus Christ.
37. I receive the anointing to rise up from the prison of financial struggle. I refuse to give up, in the name of Jesus Christ.
38. I receive the anointing to rise up from the prison of low self-esteem. I refuse to give up, in the name of Jesus Christ.
39. I receive the anointing to rise up from the prison of demonic attack. I refuse to give up, in the name of Jesus Christ.
40. I receive the anointing to rise up from the prison of business failure. I refuse to give up, in the name of Jesus Christ.
41. I receive the anointing to rise up from the prison of financial failure. I refuse to give up, in the name of Jesus Christ.
42. I receive the anointing to rise up from the prison of retrogression. I refuse to give up, in the name of Jesus Christ.
43. I receive the anointing to rise up from the prison of marital failure. I refuse to give up, in the name of Jesus Christ.
44. I receive the anointing to rise up from the prison of marital struggle. I refuse to give up, in the name of Jesus Christ.
45. I receive the anointing to rise up from the prison of ministerial failure. I refuse to give up, in the name of Jesus Christ.
46. I receive the anointing to rise up from the prison of financial rollercoaster. I refuse to give up, in the name of Jesus Christ.

47. I receive the anointing to rise up from the prison of backwardness. I refuse to give up, in the name of Jesus Christ.
48. I receive the anointing to rise up from the prison of stagnation. I refuse to give up, in the name of Jesus Christ.
49. I receive the anointing and wisdom to escape Egyptian slavery, in the name of Jesus Christ.
50. By the authority and power in the name of Jesus Christ, I am delivered from the hands of evil taskmasters, in the name of Jesus Christ.
51. I receive the anointing and wisdom to escape the wrath of Herod of my father's house, in the name of Jesus Christ.
52. I receive the anointing and wisdom to escape from the prison of household wickedness, in the name of Jesus Christ.
53. I receive the anointing and power to destroy my goliath. I claim complete victory in every area of my life, in the name of Jesus Christ.
54. I receive the anointing, power, and wisdom to cross my Red Sea, in the name of Jesus Christ.
55. By the authority and power given unto me, I command Red Sea in my life to give way now. I am crossing over to the promise land, in the name of Jesus Christ.
56. I receive the anointing, power, and wisdom to cross my river Jordan, in the name of Jesus Christ.
57. I will not die in the wilderness. I will make it to my promise land, in the name of Jesus Christ.
58. I receive the anointing, power, and wisdom to overcome every wilderness situation in my life, in the name of Jesus Christ.

59. I receive the anointing, power, and wisdom to overcome every wilderness situation in my marriage, in the name of Jesus Christ.
60. I receive the anointing, power, and wisdom to overcome every wilderness situation in my ministry, in the name of Jesus Christ.
61. I receive the anointing, power, and wisdom to overcome every wilderness situation in my finances, in the name of Jesus Christ.
62. I receive the anointing, power, and wisdom to overcome every wilderness situation in my business, in the name of Jesus Christ.
63. I receive the anointing, power, and wisdom to overcome every wilderness situation in my career, in the name of Jesus Christ.

I cover my prayers in the blood of Jesus Christ. According to the Word of God, I have asked; I shall receive. I have knocked the door; it shall be opened unto me. I have sought; I shall find, in the name of Jesus Christ. It is written, "... Decree a thing, and it shall be established". As I have spoken in prayer, it shall be so. My prayers shall produce desired results. My prayers shall produce desired miracles. My prayers shall produce desired testimonies, in the name of Jesus Christ. Territorial spirit and power cannot hinder this prayer. Sins and flesh cannot hinder this prayer. It is done. It is sealed by the blood of Jesus Christ. It is delivered to me, in Jesus mighty name. Amen!

DAY TWO

PRAYER TO STEP INTO TOTAL VICTORY

Passages To Read Before You Pray:
Revelation 12:11, 1 John 5:4-8, 2 Chronicles 20:15, Psalms 3, 9, 35, 68, 70, 140

In the book of Job 22:28, the Scripture says when I decree a thing, it shall be established for me. I stand on this Scripture and decree. I have come into the presence of God today to plead my case. I enter through the gate of praise into the sanctuary of heaven. I cover myself in the precious blood of Jesus Christ. I baptize myself in the fire of the Holy Ghost. I charge this atmosphere with the fire of God, and I take this neighborhood for the Lord. I arrest every principality and power, territorial spirit, and every throne and kingdom that is not of God. I cast you down and I command you never to lift yourself up against me, because I have the life of God in me.

In the name of Jesus Christ, I confess my sins today, and I ask you O Lord to forgive me on the basis of your mercy. With all my heart, I forgive those who have sinned against me from the past through this moment. I release them from any form of guilt and shame, in the name of Jesus Christ. I hereby plead the blood of Jesus over any sins committed by my parents and ancestors. I cancel through the Blood of Jesus Christ, any satanic covenants, exchanges, vows or transactions made over my life, body, soul, spirit, and circumstances, in the name of Jesus Christ. I cancel every legal right that the devil may have against me, by the blood of Jesus Christ. The accuser of the brethren will have nothing against me as I come to the presence of God in prayer.

The devil cannot hinder or delay my prayer, because I know who I am. I am a child of the Kingdom; I am a king and priest of the Lord, redeemed from the hand of the devil by the blood of Jesus Christ. I declare that all satanic thrones, altars, dominions, principalities, powers, rulers of darkness, queen of the coast, queen of heavens, household wickedness, spiritual hosts of wickedness and all satanic works, have no power or authority over my life. I declare that satanic harassment and intimidation have no effect on me.

Today I receive divine strength to pray; I will not pray in vain. I will not pray amiss. My prayers will bring the desired results. I command the fountain of prayer to open now, and flow into my life, I command the warring angels of God to descend and fight on my behalf. Every minute and every hour that I spend in prayer will bring solution. Every prayer point will attract divine attention and divine intervention. I decree open heavens over my prayers, and today, God of heaven and earth will attend to my case. My prayers today will shake the heavens and move the earth; testimonies, miracles, healing, breakthrough, signs and wonders will follow my prayers. At the end of this prayer session, my life will never be the same again.

PRAYER POINTS

1. O God my Father, thank you for being my God, my Father and my friend.
2. O God my Father, thank you for the privilege to know you and the power of the resurrection of Jesus Christ.
3. O God my Father, thank you for always being there for me and with me.

4. O God my Father, thank you for the great and mighty things that you are doing in my life.
5. O God my Father, thank you for your provision and protection over me and my household.
6. O God my Father, thank you for always answering my prayers.
7. I confess my sins before you today and I ask you to forgive me on the basis of your mercy, in the name of Jesus Christ.
8. Wash me clean today O Lord by the blood of Jesus Christ.
9. I cover myself and my household with the blood of Jesus Christ.
10. My prayers today will not go in vain; my prayers will produce the desired results in the name of Jesus Christ.
11. I cancel every satanic decree issued to torment me, in the name of Jesus Christ.
12. I cancel every satanic decree issued to stop my progress, in the name of Jesus Christ.
13. I cancel every satanic decree issued to delay my promotion, in the name of Jesus Christ.
14. I cancel every satanic decree issued to afflict me and my family, in the name of Jesus Christ.
15. I arrest every satanic agent assigned to set me back. I bind and cast you down into the pit of hell, in the name of Jesus Christ.
16. By the power in the blood of Jesus Christ, I command my gates of breakthroughs to open now, in the name of Jesus Christ.
17. By the power in the blood of Jesus Christ, I command my gates of financial freedom to open now, in the name of Jesus Christ.

18. By the power in the blood of Jesus Christ, I command my gates of sudden miracles to open now, in the name of Jesus Christ.
19. By the power in the blood of Jesus Christ, I command my gates of prosperity to open now, in the name of Jesus Christ.
20. Any sickness that wants to destroy my life, I command you to disappear, in the name of Jesus Christ.
21. Any sickness that wants to control my life, I command you to disappear, in the name of Jesus Christ.
22. Any sickness assigned to kill me, I command you to disappear, in the name of Jesus Christ.
23. Any sickness assigned to delay what God is doing in my life, I command you to disappear, in the name of Jesus Christ.
24. Any sickness assigned to hinder my divine acceleration, I command you to disappear, in the name of Jesus Christ.
25. By the power in the blood of Jesus Christ, I receive power to rule over my environment, in the name of Jesus Christ.
26. By the power in the blood of Jesus Christ, I receive power to rule over my territory, in the name of Jesus Christ.
27. By the authority and power in the blood of Jesus Christ, I step into sudden wealth, in the name of Jesus Christ.
28. Any power anywhere coming from behind to steal from me, I command you to be buried alive, in the name of Jesus Christ.
29. Any power anywhere coming to rob me of my miracle, you will not escape the judgment of God, in the name of Jesus Christ.

30. O God my Father, arise and connect me to my timing, in the name of Jesus Christ.
31. I receive the anointing of the sons of Issachar, to recognize my moment of divine appointment, in the name of Jesus Christ.
32. I receive the anointing of the sons of Issachar, to recognize my moment of miracle, in the name of Jesus Christ.
33. I receive the anointing of the sons of Issachar, to recognize my moment of transformation, in the name of Jesus Christ.
34. O God my Father, arise and connect me to my destiny, in the name of Jesus Christ.
35. O God my Father, arise and connect me to the people who will help me, in the name of Jesus Christ.
36. O God my Father, arise and connect me to my Joseph who will interpret my dreams, in the name of Jesus Christ.
37. O God my Father, arise and connect me to my Moses who will confront and conquer my Pharaoh, in the name of Jesus Christ.
38. O God my Father, arise and connect me to my Moses who will rescue me from the bondage of Egypt, in the name of Jesus Christ.
39. O God my Father, arise and connect me to my Moses who will command the Red Sea to give way for me to cross to the other side, in the name of Jesus Christ.
40. O God my Father, arise and connect me to my Moses who will bring water out of the rock for me, in the name of Jesus Christ.

41. O God my Father, arise and connect me to my Moses who will turn bitterness to sweetness in my life, in the name of Jesus Christ.
42. O God my Father, arise and connect me to my Joshua who will bring down the walls of Jericho hindering my breakthroughs, in the name of Jesus Christ.
43. O God my Father, arise and connect me to my David who will kill my Goliath, in the name of Jesus Christ.
44. O God my Father, arise and connect me to the people in high places, in the name of Jesus Christ.
45. O God my Father, arise and connect me to rulers and lawmakers of this land, in the name of Jesus Christ.
46. Evil pronouncement released to keep me at the bottom of the ladder, I command you to lose authority over my life, in the name of Jesus Christ.
47. Evil pronouncement released to keep me in bondage, I command you to loose your hold over my life, in the name of Jesus Christ.
48. Evil pronouncement released to keep me in poverty, I command you to loose your grip over me, in the name of Jesus Christ.
49. O God my Father, arise and release your wrath upon every power of witchcraft troubling my destiny, in the name of Jesus Christ.
50. O God my Father, arise and release your wrath upon every power of witchcraft troubling my life, in the name of Jesus Christ.
51. O God my Father, arise and release your wrath upon every power of witchcraft troubling my family, in the name of Jesus Christ.

52. O God my Father, arise and release your wrath upon every power of witchcraft troubling my spouse, in the name of Jesus Christ.
53. O God my Father, arise and release your wrath upon every power of witchcraft troubling my children, in the name of Jesus Christ.
54. O God my Father, arise and release your wrath upon every power of witchcraft troubling my finances, in the name of Jesus Christ.
55. O God my Father, arise and release your wrath upon every power of witchcraft troubling my ministry, in the name of Jesus Christ.
56. O God my Father, arise and release your wrath upon every power of witchcraft troubling my business, in the name of Jesus Christ.
57. O God my Father, arise and release your wrath upon every power of witchcraft troubling me in my dream, in the name of Jesus Christ.
58. I release panic and havoc upon the camp of my enemy, in the name of Jesus Christ.
59. I release confusion and backwardness upon the camp of household wickedness, in the name of Jesus Christ.
60. I release the ten plagues of Egypt upon every agent of darkness tormenting my existence, in the name of Jesus Christ.
61. I release the ten plagues of Egypt upon every agent of darkness tormenting my life, in the name of Jesus Christ.
62. I release the ten plagues of Egypt upon every agent of darkness tormenting my family, in the name of Jesus Christ.

63. Any power anywhere putting me in the right place at the wrong time, I command you to loose your hold over life, in the name of Jesus Christ.
64. Any power anywhere causing me to make mistakes at the point of breakthrough, I command you to loose your hold over my life, in the name of Jesus Christ.
65. Any power anywhere repeating evil cycles in my life, I command you to loose your hold over my life, in the name of Jesus Christ.
66. By the power and authority in the blood of Jesus Christ, I command every evil cycle in my life to break, in the name of Jesus Christ.
67. Every ancestral problem of one day late in my life, break by the fire of God, in the name of Jesus Christ.
68. Every ancestral problem of one dollar short in my life, break by the fire of God, in the name of Jesus Christ.
69. Every ancestral problem of failure by one point in my life, break by the fire of God, in the name of Jesus Christ.
70. Every ancestral problem of too little, too late in my life, break now by the fire of God, in the name of Jesus Christ.

I cover my prayers in the blood of Jesus Christ. According to the Word of God, I have asked, I shall receive. I have knocked the door, it shall be opened unto me. I have sought, I shall find, in the name of Jesus Christ. It is written, "… Decree a thing, and it shall be established". As I have spoken in prayer, it shall be so. My prayers shall produce desire results. My prayers shall produce desired miracles. My prayers shall produce desired testimonies, in the name of Jesus Christ. Territorial spirit and power cannot hinder this prayer. Sins and flesh cannot hinder this prayer. It is done. It is sealed by the blood of Jesus Christ. It is delivered to me, in Jesus might name. Amen!

DAY THREE

I REFUSE TO COOPERATE

Passages To Read Before You Pray:
Psalms 3, 34, 35, 94, 106

In the book of Job 22:28, the Scripture says when I decree a thing, it shall be established for me. I stand on this Scripture and decree. I have come into the presence of God today to plead my case. I enter through the gate of praise into the sanctuary of heaven. I cover myself in the precious blood of Jesus Christ. I baptize myself in the fire of the Holy Ghost. I charge this atmosphere with the fire of God, and I take this neighborhood for the Lord. I arrest every principality and power, territorial spirit, and every throne and kingdom that is not of God. I cast you down and I command you never to lift yourself up against me, because I have the life of God in me.

In the name of Jesus Christ, I confess my sins today, and I ask you O Lord to forgive me on the basis of your mercy. With all my heart, I forgive those who have sinned against me from the past through this moment. I release them from any form of guilt and shame, in the name of Jesus Christ. I hereby plead the blood of Jesus over any sins committed by my parents and ancestors. I cancel through the Blood of Jesus Christ, any satanic covenants, exchanges, vows or transactions made over my life, body, soul, spirit, and circumstances, in the name of Jesus Christ. I cancel every legal right that the devil may have against me, by the blood of Jesus Christ. The accuser of the brethren will have nothing against me as I come to the presence of God in prayer.

The devil cannot hinder or delay my prayer, because I know who I am. I am a child of the Kingdom; I am a king and priest of the

Lord, redeemed from the hand of the devil by the blood of Jesus Christ. I declare that all satanic thrones, altars, dominions, principalities, powers, rulers of darkness, queen of the coast, queen of heavens, household wickedness, spiritual hosts of wickedness and all satanic works, have no power or authority over my life. I declare that satanic harassment and intimidation have no effect on me.

Today I receive divine strength to pray; I will not pray in vain. I will not pray amiss. My prayers will bring the desired results. I command the fountain of prayer to open now, and flow into my life, I command the warring angels of God to descend and fight on my behalf. Every minute and every hour that I spend in prayer will bring solution. Every prayer point will attract divine attention and divine intervention. I decree open heavens over my prayers, and today, God of heaven and earth will attend to my case. My prayers today will shake the heavens and move the earth; testimonies, miracles, healing, breakthrough, signs and wonders will follow my prayers. At the end of this prayer session, my life will never be the same again.

PRAYER POINTS

1. O God my Father, thank you for being my God, my Father and my friend.
2. O God my Father, thank you for the privilege to know you and the power of the resurrection of Jesus Christ.
3. O God my Father, thank you for always being there for me and with me.
4. O God my Father, thank you for the great and mighty things that you are doing in my life.

5. O God my Father, thank you for your provision and protection over me and my household.
6. O God my Father, thank you for always answering my prayers.
7. I confess my sins before you today and I ask you to forgive me on the basis of your mercy, in the name of Jesus Christ.
8. Wash me clean today O Lord by the blood of Jesus Christ.
9. I cover myself and my household with the blood of Jesus Christ.
10. My prayers today will not go in vain; my prayers will produce the desired results in the name of Jesus Christ.
11. I refuse to cooperate with the power that wants to destroy my life.
12. I refuse to cooperate with the power that wants to destroy my future.
13. I refuse to cooperate with the power that wants to destroy my vision.
14. I refuse to cooperate with the power that wants to destroy my dream.
15. I refuse to cooperate with the power that wants to destroy my finances.
16. I refuse to cooperate with the power that wants to rob me of my blessings.
17. I refuse to cooperate with the power that is holding me captive.
18. I refuse to cooperate with the power that wants to destroy my destiny.
19. I refuse to cooperate with the plan of the enemies to change my destiny.

20. I refuse to cooperate with the power of the enemies fighting against my prayer.
21. Father Lord, let the plan of the enemy fail over my life.
22. Father Lord, let the plan of the enemy fail over my household.
23. Father Lord, let the plan of the enemy fail over my future.
24. Father Lord, let the plan of the enemy fail over my finances.
25. Father Lord, let the plan of the enemy fail over my destiny.
26. Every evil arrow shot at me by the enemy, go back to sender.
27. Every arrow of sudden death shot at me by the enemy, go back to sender.
28. Every arrow of sudden destruction shot at me by the enemy, go back to your sender.
29. Every arrow of sickness shot at me by the enemy, go back to sender.
30. Every arrow of failure shot at me by the enemy, go back to sender.
31. Father Lord, let your angel of destruction go through the camp of my enemies.
32. The expectation of the enemy over my life shall not stand.
33. The expectation of the enemy over my job/business shall not stand.
34. The expectation of the enemy over my ministry shall not stand.
35. The expectation of the enemy over my future shall not stand.

36. The expectation of the enemy over my dream shall not stand.
37. The expectation of the enemy over my purpose in life shall not stand.
38. The expectation of the enemy over my finances shall not stand.
39. The expectation of the enemy over my household shall not stand.
40. I shall laugh last over the enemy of my soul.
41. I shall laugh last over the enemy of my progress.
42. I shall laugh last over the enemy of my promotion.
43. I shall laugh last over the enemy of my success.
44. I shall laugh last over the enemy of my breakthroughs.
45. I shall laugh last over the enemy of my life.
46. I shall laugh last over the enemy of my dreams.
47. I shall laugh last over the enemy of my vision.
48. Enemy that refuses to give up on my life shall die before his time.
49. Enemy that refuses to give up on my breakthrough, die before your time.
50. I receive anointing to overcome every problem of life.
51. I receive anointing to overcome every financial problem in my life.
52. Father Lord, take away the power of boasters boasting over my life.
53. Father Lord, take away the power of boasters boasting over my success.
54. Father Lord, take away the power of boasters boasting over my household.
55. Father Lord, take away the power of boasters boasting over my breakthroughs.

56. Father Lord, take away the power of boasters boasting over my achievements.
57. Father Lord, take away the power of boasters boasting over my future.
58. I refuse to quit and I command my enemies to surrender.
59. I refuse to quit and I command my blessings to manifest by fire.
60. I refuse to quit and I command my helpers to locate me by fire.
61. I refuse to quit and I command my breakthroughs to come by fire.
62. I refuse to quit and I command my promotion to come by fire.
63. I refuse to quit and I command my stars to shine by fire.

I cover my prayers in the blood of Jesus Christ. According to the Word of God, I have asked, I shall receive. I have knocked the door, it shall be opened unto me. I have sought, I shall find, in the name of Jesus Christ. It is written, "… Decree a thing, and it shall be established". As I have spoken in prayer, it shall be so. My prayers shall produce desire results. My prayers shall produce desired miracles. My prayers shall produce desired testimonies, in the name of Jesus Christ. Territorial spirit and power cannot hinder this prayer. Sins and flesh cannot hinder this prayer. It is done. It is sealed by the blood of Jesus Christ. It is delivered to me, in Jesus might name. Amen!

DAY FOUR

WAR AGAINST SATANIC CONTRACTORS

Passages To Read Before You Pray:
Numbers 22:1-12, Isaiah 8:9-10, Psalms 3, 2, 68, 83, 109

In the book of Job 22:28, the Scripture says when I decree a thing, it shall be established for me. I stand on this Scripture and decree. I have come into the presence of God today to plead my case. I enter through the gate of praise, into the sanctuary of heaven. I cover myself in the precious blood of Jesus Christ. I baptize myself in the fire of the Holy Ghost. I charge this atmosphere with the fire of God, and I take this neighborhood for the Lord. I arrest every principality and power, territorial spirit, and every throne and kingdom that is not of God. I cast you down and I command you never to lift yourself up against me, because I have the life of God in me.

In the name of Jesus Christ, I confess my sins today, and I ask you O Lord to forgive me on the basis of your mercy. With all my heart, I forgive those who have sinned against me; from the past through this moment. I release them from any form of guilt and shame, in the name of Jesus Christ. I hereby plead the blood of Jesus over any sins committed by my parents and ancestors. I cancel through the Blood of Jesus Christ, any satanic covenants, exchanges, vows or transactions, made over my life, body, soul, spirit, and circumstances, in the name of Jesus Christ. I cancel every legal right that the devil may have against me, by the blood of Jesus Christ. The accuser of the brethren will have nothing against me, as I come to the presence of God in prayer.

The devil cannot hinder or delay my prayer, because I know who I am. I am a child of the Kingdom. I am a king and priest of the

Lord, redeemed from the hand of the devil by the blood of Jesus Christ. I walk in power. I walk in miracle. Proverbs 18:21 says, death and life are in the power of my tongue; I command the power in my tongue to manifest now. I command my tongue to become fire, to consume all the powers of darkness in the air, the land, the sea, and beneath the earth. I hereby raise Holy Ghost standard against the prince of the power of the air and all the hosts of darkness in the air. I raise Holy Ghost standard against the queen of the coasts and all the hosts of darkness on the land. I raise Holy Ghost standard against the marine kingdom and all the hosts of darkness in the sea. I raise Holy Ghost standard against the kingdom of hell and all the hosts of darkness beneath the earth. I shoot down all the networks of demons gathering to resist my prayers. I rebuke and bind all the controlling forces of darkness standing against my prayers.

I declare that all satanic thrones, altars, dominions, principalities, powers, rulers of darkness, queens of the coast, queens of heavens, household wickedness, spiritual hosts of wickedness and all satanic works, have no power or authority over my life. I declare that satanic harassment and intimidation have no effect on me.

Today, I receive divine strength to pray; I will not pray in vain. I will not pray amiss. My prayers will bring the desired results. I command the fountain of prayer to open now, and to flow into my life, I command the warring angels of God to descend and fight on my behalf. Every minute and every hour that I spend in prayer, will bring solution. Every prayer point will attract divine attention and divine intervention. I decree open heavens over my prayers, and today, God of heaven and earth will attend to my case. My prayers today will shake the heavens and move the earth. Testimonies, miracles, healings, breakthroughs, and signs and wonders, will follow my prayers. At the end of this prayer session, my life will never be the same again.

PRAYER POINTS

1. O God my Father, thank you for being my God, my Father and my friend.
2. O God my Father, thank you for the privilege to know you and the power of the resurrection of Jesus Christ.
3. O God my Father, thank you for always being there for me and with me.
4. O God my Father, thank you for the great and mighty things that you are doing in my life.
5. O God my Father, thank you for your provision and protection over me and my household.
6. O God my Father, thank you for always answering my prayers.
7. I confess my sins before you today and I ask you to forgive me on the basis of your mercy, in the name of Jesus Christ.
8. Wash me clean today O Lord by the blood of Jesus Christ.
9. I cover myself and my household with the blood of Jesus Christ.
10. My prayers today will not go in vain; my prayers will produce the desired results in the name of Jesus Christ.
11. Representatives of hell that will not let me have peace at work, O God my Father, let the whirlwind of God violently blow them away, in the name of Jesus Christ.

12. Representatives of hell that will not let me have peace at home, O God my Father, let the whirlwind of God violently blow them away, in the name of Jesus Christ.
13. Representatives of hell that will not let me have peace in my neighborhood, O God my Father, let the whirlwind of God violently blow them away, in the name of Jesus Christ.
14. Representatives of hell that will not let me have peace in my family, O God my Father, let the whirlwind of God violently blow them away, in the name of Jesus Christ.
15. Representatives of hell that will not let me have peace among my friends, O God my Father, let the whirlwind of God violently blow them away, in the name of Jesus Christ.
16. Satanic contractors sent to rob me of my God given blessings, O God my Father, let the whirlwind of God violently blow them away, in the name of Jesus Christ.
17. Satanic contractors sent to monitor my outgoing and incoming, O God my Father, let the whirlwind of God violently blow them away, in the name of Jesus Christ.
18. Satanic contractors sent to cause confusion in my marriage, O God my Father, let the whirlwind of God violently blow them away, in the name of Jesus Christ.
19. Satanic contractors sent to make my life miserable, O God my Father, let the whirlwind of God violently blow them away, in the name of Jesus Christ.
20. Satanic contractors sent to make success impossible for me, O God my Father, let the whirlwind of God violently blow them away, in the name of Jesus Christ.
21. Satanic contractors sent to make breakthroughs impossible for me, O God my Father, let the whirlwind

of God violently blow them away, in the name of Jesus Christ.

22. Satanic contractors sent to infect me with sickness, O God my Father, let the whirlwind of God violently blow them away, in the name of Jesus Christ.

23. Satanic contractors sent to make it impossible for me to move forward in life, O God my Father, let the whirlwind of God violently blow them away, in the name of Jesus Christ.

24. Satanic contractors sent to pollute my prayer altar, O God my Father, let the whirlwind of God violently blow them away, in the name of Jesus Christ.

25. Satanic contractors sent to prolong my problems, O God my Father, let the whirlwind of God violently blow them away, in the name of Jesus Christ.

26. Satanic contractors sent to add affliction to afflictions in my life, O God my Father, let the whirlwind of God violently blow them away, in the name of Jesus Christ.

27. Satanic contractors sent to keep me in bondage, O God my Father, let the whirlwind of God violently blow them away, in the name of Jesus Christ.

28. Satanic contractors acting as my friends in order to get close to me, O God my Father, expose them and let the whirlwind of God violently blow them away, in the name of Jesus Christ.

29. Satanic contractors sent to hinder my prayers, enough is enough. O Lord, let the whirlwind of God violently blow them away, in the name of Jesus Christ.

30. Satanic contractors sent to corrupt my anointing, O God my Father, let the whirlwind violently blow them away, in the name of Jesus Christ.

31. Satanic contractors sent to keep me stagnated, enough is enough. O Lord, let the whirlwind of God violently blow them away, in the name of Jesus Christ.
32. Satanic contractors sent to abort my pregnancy of good things, O God my Father, let the whirlwind of God violently blow them away, in the name of Jesus Christ.
33. Satanic contractors sent to drive my helpers away from me, enough is enough. O Lord, let the whirlwind of God violently blow them away, in the name of Jesus Christ.
34. Satanic contractors sent to renew my solved problems, O God my Father this is not allowed, let the whirlwind of God violently blow them away, in the name of Jesus Christ.
35. Satanic contractors sent to kill me before my time, I will not die but live. O God my Father, let the whirlwind of God violently blow them away, in the name of Jesus Christ.

I cover my prayers in the blood of Jesus Christ. According to the Word of God, I have asked; I shall receive. I have knocked the door; it shall be opened unto me. I have sought; I shall find, in the name of Jesus Christ. It is written, "... Decree a thing, and it shall be established". As I have spoken in prayer, it shall be so. My prayers shall produce desired results. My prayers shall produce desired miracles. My prayers shall produce desired testimonies, in the name of Jesus Christ. Territorial spirit and power cannot hinder this prayer. Sins and flesh cannot hinder this prayer. It is done. It is sealed by the blood of Jesus Christ. It is delivered to me, in Jesus mighty name. Amen!

DAY FIVE

PRAYER TO OVERCOME OBSTACLES IN YOUR WAY

Passages To Read Before You Pray:
Exodus 14:1-14, Isaiah 45:2-3, Psalms 46, 10, 118

In the book of Job 22:28, the Scripture says when I decree a thing, it shall be established for me. I stand on this Scripture and decree. I have come today to fellowship with my heavenly Father, and make my requests and needs known unto Him. I cannot be hindered nor delayed because I know who I am in the Lord. I am a child of the Kingdom, born of the Spirit, redeemed by the blood of Jesus Christ. I walk in authority, living life without any apology because the power and authority has been given to me according to the Word of God in the book of Luke 9:1.

As I have come to pray today and to fellowship with my heavenly Father, I cover myself in the blood of Jesus Christ, and I put on the whole armor of God. I hereby come against every Prince of Persia that wants to hinder my prayer, I arrest you by the power in the blood of Jesus Christ, and I bind you and cast you down into the pit of hell.

I come against principalities and powers that wrestle with me and my prayers, I arrest you today by the power in the name of Jesus Christ, and I bind you and cast down into the pit of hell. I come against the rulers of the darkness of this world, against spiritual wickedness in high places, I arrest you all by the power in the name of Jesus Christ, and I bind you and cast you down into the pit of hell. I come against weakness and weariness, I arrest you today by the power in the name of Jesus Christ, and I bind you and cast you out of my life. I come against wondering spirit and distractions, I arrest you today by the power in the name of Jesus Christ, and I bind you and cast you out of my life.

Today I receive the anointing to pray and get results, my prayers cannot be hindered nor delayed because Jesus is my Lord, I will pray today and get the desired results, I decree open heavens upon my prayers. I baptize myself in the fire of the Holy Ghost; therefore I have become too hot for the enemy to handle. My prayers today will attract divine intervention to every situation in my life; signs and wonders will follow my prayers today, testimonies will follow my prayers today and the name of God alone will be glorified, in Jesus name. Amen!

PRAYER POINTS:

1. O God my Father, thank you for being my God, my Father and my friend.
2. O God my Father, thank you for the privilege to know you and the power of the resurrection of Jesus Christ.
3. O God my Father, thank you for always being there for me and with me.
4. O God my Father, thank you for the great and mighty things that you are doing in my life.
5. O God my Father, thank you for your provision and protection over me and my household.
6. O God my Father, thank you for always answering my prayers.
7. I confess my sins before you today and I ask you to forgive me on the basis of your mercy, in the name of Jesus Christ.

8. Wash me clean today O Lord by the blood of Jesus Christ.
9. I cover myself and my household with the blood of Jesus Christ.
10. My prayers today will not go in vain; my prayers will produce the desired results in the name of Jesus Christ.
11. By the power in the name of Jesus Christ, I command Red Sea on my way to give way right now, I am crossing over.
12. By the power in the name of Jesus Christ, I command every Red Sea that wants to keep me in the Egyptian bondage, to dry up.
13. By the power in the name of Jesus Christ, I command every Red Sea that wants me to die in Egypt to give way now.
14. By the power in the name of Jesus Christ, I command the Red Sea on my way to swallow my stubborn pursuers.
15. O God my Father, send the east wind today and divide the Red Sea on my way so that I may cross over to my promise land.
16. O ye Red Sea on the way to my promise land, I command you to cooperate with the divine agenda for my life.
17. O ye Red Sea on the way to my promise land, you cannot stop me I am a child of the King, give way now.
18. O ye Red Sea on the way to my promise land, you cannot hinder me I am a child of the King, give way now.
19. O ye Red Sea on the way to my promise land, you cannot delay me I am a child of the King, give way now.

20. Any power anywhere expecting me to die in the wilderness of hopelessness, you will not escape the judgment of God. (Ex. 14:3)
21. Any power anywhere expecting me to die in the wilderness of problem, you will not escape the judgment of God.
22. Any power anywhere expecting me to die in the wilderness of poverty, you will not escape the judgment of God.
23. Any power anywhere expecting me to die in the wilderness of suffering, you will not escape the judgment of God.
24. Any power anywhere expecting me to die in the wilderness of confusion, you will not escape the judgment of God.
25. Any power anywhere expecting me to die in the wilderness of ignorance, you will not escape the judgment of God.
26. Any power anywhere expecting me to die in the wilderness of sadness and bitterness, you will not escape the judgment of God.
27. Any power anywhere expecting me to die in the wilderness of lack, you will not escape the judgment of God.
28. Any power anywhere pursuing me in order to enslave me, fall today, you and your army in the order of Pharaoh. (Ex. 14:5-9)
29. Any power anywhere pursuing me in order to destroy the works of my hand, fall today, you and your army in the order of Pharaoh.

30. Household wickedness pursuing me in order to hinder the plan of God for my life, you will not escape the judgment of God.
31. Anybody anywhere pursuing me in order to stop what God is doing in my life, be disappointed today because you cannot stop God.
32. Anybody anywhere pursuing me in order to fulfill his desire upon my life, I command you to fail, my case is different.
33. O God my Father, when I am confused and don't know what to do, let there be divine intervention in every area of my life.
34. O God my Father, when all hope is lost and my faith is weak, arise and carry me in your arm.
35. O God my Father, when I am weak and don't have the strength to pray, let your grace be sufficient for me.
36. O God my Father, when all roads are closed and darkness covers my way, let your light shine and make a way where there seems to be no way.
37. O God my Father, deliver me today from the hands of Pharaoh that wants to keep me in bondage.
38. No matter the situation around me, I will not die in Egypt.
39. Arise O Lord and sign my release form today, I am getting out of this bondage.
40. Arise O Lord and sign my release form today, I am getting out of this stubborn situation.
41. Arise O Lord and sign my release form today, I am getting out of this hopeless situation.
42. Arise O Lord and sign my release form today, I am getting out of this problem.

43. Arise O Lord and sign my release form today, I am getting out of this financial mess.
44. Arise O Lord and sign my release form today, I am getting out of this shameful situation.
45. Arise O Lord and sign my release form today, I am getting out of this wilderness.
46. As I lift up my voice in prayer today, let my stubborn situation tremble and bow at the name of Jesus Christ. (James 2:19)(Philippians 2:9-11)
47. As I lift up my voice in prayer today, let my stubborn enemy tremble and bow at the name of Jesus Christ.
48. As I lift up my voice in prayer today, let my household wickedness tremble and bow at the name of Jesus Christ.
49. As I lift up my voice in prayer today, let the power assigned to hinder my prayers tremble and bow at the name of Jesus Christ.
50. As I lift up my voice in prayer today, let the power assigned to stop my breakthrough tremble and bow at the name of Jesus Christ.
51. As I lift up my voice in prayer today, let the power assigned to delay my promotion tremble and bow at the name of Jesus Christ.
52. As I lift up my voice in prayer today, let the power assigned to attack my joy tremble and bow at the name of Jesus Christ.
53. As I lift up my voice in prayer today, let the power assigned to my marriage tremble and bow at the name of Jesus Christ.
54. As I lift up my voice in prayer today, let the power assigned to attack my finances tremble and bow at the name of Jesus Christ.

55. As I lift up my voice in prayer today, let the power of sickness in my life tremble and bow at the name of Jesus Christ.
56. As I lift up my voice in prayer today, let the power of poverty in my life tremble and bow at the name of Jesus Christ.
57. Today O Lord, let every mountain of problem in my life disappear.
58. Today O Lord, let every ocean of problem in my life disappear.
59. Today O Lord, let every wilderness of problem in my life disappear.
60. Today O Lord, let every cloud of problem over my life clear away.

I cover my prayers in the blood of Jesus Christ. According to the Word of God, I have asked, I shall receive. I have knocked the door, it shall be opened unto me. I have sought, I shall find, in the name of Jesus Christ. It is written, "… Decree a thing, and it shall be established". As I have spoken in prayer, it shall be so. My prayers shall produce desire results. My prayers shall produce desired miracles. My prayers shall produce desired testimonies, in the name of Jesus Christ. Territorial spirit and power cannot hinder this prayer. Sins and flesh cannot hinder this prayer. It is done. It is sealed by the blood of Jesus Christ. It is delivered to me, in Jesus might name. Amen!

DAY SIX

PRAYER AGAINST OPPOSITION

Passages to read before you pray:
Isaiah 8:9-10, 2 Chronicles 20:1-29,
Psalms 68, 3, 35, 27, 107

In the book of Job 22:28, the Scripture says when I decree a thing, it shall be established for me. I stand on this Scripture and decree. I have come into the presence of God today to plead my case. I enter through the gate of praise into the sanctuary of heaven. I cover myself in the precious blood of Jesus Christ. I baptize myself in the fire of the Holy Ghost. I charge this atmosphere with the fire of God, and I take this neighborhood for the Lord. I arrest every principality and power, territorial spirit, and every throne and kingdom that is not of God. I cast you down and I command you never to lift yourself up against me, because I have the life of God in me.

In the name of Jesus Christ, I confess my sins today, and I ask you O Lord to forgive me on the basis of your mercy. With all my heart, I forgive those who have sinned against me from the past through this moment. I release them from any form of guilt and shame, in the name of Jesus Christ. I hereby plead the blood of Jesus over any sins committed by my parents and ancestors. I cancel through the Blood of Jesus Christ, any satanic covenants, exchanges, vows or transactions made over my life, body, soul, spirit, and circumstances, in the name of Jesus Christ. I cancel every legal right that the devil may have against me, by the blood of Jesus Christ. The accuser of the brethren will have nothing against me as I come to the presence of God in prayer.

The devil cannot hinder or delay my prayer, because I know who I am. I am a child of the Kingdom; I am a king and priest of the Lord, redeemed from the hand of the devil by the blood of Jesus Christ. I declare that all satanic thrones, altars, dominions, principalities, powers, rulers of darkness, queen of the coast, queen of heavens, household wickedness, spiritual hosts of wickedness and all satanic works, have no power or authority over my life. I declare that satanic harassment and intimidation have no effect on me.

Today I receive divine strength to pray; I will not pray in vain. I will not pray amiss. My prayers will bring the desired results. I command the fountain of prayer to open now, and flow into my life, I command the warring angels of God to descend and fight on my behalf. Every minute and every hour that I spend in prayer will bring solution. Every prayer point will attract divine attention and divine intervention. I decree open heavens over my prayers, and today, God of heaven and earth will attend to my case. My prayers today will shake the heavens and move the earth; testimonies, miracles, healing, breakthrough, signs and wonders will follow my prayers. At the end of this prayer session, my life will never be the same again.

PRAYER POINTS

1. O God my Father, thank you for being my God, my Father and my friend.
2. O God my Father, thank you for the privilege to know you and the power of the resurrection of Jesus Christ.
3. O God my Father, thank you for always being there for me and with me.

4. O God my Father, thank you for the great and mighty things that you are doing in my life.
5. O God my Father, thank you for your provision and protection over me and my household.
6. O God my Father, thank you for always answering my prayers.
7. I confess my sins before you today and I ask you to forgive me on the basis of your mercy, in the name of Jesus Christ.
8. Wash me clean today O Lord by the blood of Jesus Christ.
9. I cover myself and my household with the blood of Jesus Christ.
10. My prayers today will not go in vain; my prayers will produce the desired results in the name of Jesus Christ.
11. O God my Father, thank you for the grace you have given me to be who I am; and where I am today.
12. I appreciate you O Lord, the Father of all creation, for your divine provision, protection and support.
13. O God my Father, I pray that you grant me peace, and support me on every side.
14. I receive the peace of God that is beyond human comprehension, in Jesus' name.
15. O God my Father, help me to live daily in a way pleasing to you, in Jesus' name.
16. O God my Father, change me to conform to your plan and purpose for my life, in Jesus' name.
17. O God my Father, increase my joy; and let it overflow, even in the face of opposition, in Jesus' name.
18. O God my Father, deliver me from every evil plot against my life, my prosperity and my family, in the name of Jesus Christ.

19. I wipe out every evil handwriting against my integrity, in Jesus' name.
20. I destroy every conspiracy to soil my good reputation, in Jesus' name.
21. I command Holy Ghost fire upon any person, or personality who has vowed never to see me live a peaceful life, in the name of Jesus Christ.
22. Whoever has vowed, or determined to always oppose me no-matter what I do, I release the fire of God upon you, in Jesus' name.
23. O God my Father, let the peace of anybody who is never happy to see me happy, be taken away until he/she leaves me alone, in the name of Jesus Christ.
24. Father, I decree that all those who have been fighting against me, will begin to defend and favor me from NOW, in Jesus' name.
25. O God my Father, let my enemies be at peace with me, in Jesus' name.
26. I command that all who have been in opposition to me will from now turn around, and stand for me, in Jesus' name.
27. O God my Father, raise up for me people who find joy in speaking well of me.
28. I overthrow every conspiracy to take away from me, my job, business, contract, marriage, relationship, or position, in the name of Jesus Christ.
29. I command Holy Ghost fire upon anybody who has vowed or determined to take from me at all cost; my God-given blessings, prosperity, family, or ministry, in Jesus' name.
30. I decree that all those who oppose me; if they will not repent, be removed from my life, in Jesus' name.

31. O God my Father, I pray spoil the counsel and wisdom of those who knew me well, or used to be very close to me; but now have become my enemies. Father, defeat them for me, in the name of Jesus Christ.

I cover my prayers in the blood of Jesus Christ. According to the Word of God, I have asked, I shall receive. I have knocked the door, it shall be opened unto me. I have sought, I shall find, in the name of Jesus Christ. It is written, "… Decree a thing, and it shall be established". As I have spoken in prayer, it shall be so. My prayers shall produce desire results. My prayers shall produce desired miracles. My prayers shall produce desired testimonies, in the name of Jesus Christ. Territorial spirit and power cannot hinder this prayer. Sins and flesh cannot hinder this prayer. It is done. It is sealed by the blood of Jesus Christ. It is delivered to me, in Jesus might name. Amen!

DAY SEVEN

ENOUGH IS ENOUGH

Passages To Read Before You Pray:
Psalms 30, 83, 109, Joel 2:21-24, Habakkuk 1:5

In the book of Job 22:28, the Scripture says when I decree a thing, it shall be established for me. I stand on this Scripture and decree. I have come into the presence of God today to plead my case. I enter through the gate of praise into the sanctuary of heaven. I cover myself in the precious blood of Jesus Christ. I baptize myself in the fire of the Holy Ghost. I charge this atmosphere with the fire of God, and I take this neighborhood for the Lord. I arrest every principality and power, territorial spirit, and every throne and kingdom that is not of God. I cast you down and I command you never to lift yourself up against me, because I have the life of God in me.

In the name of Jesus Christ, I confess my sins today, and I ask you O Lord to forgive me on the basis of your mercy. With all my heart, I forgive those who have sinned against me from the past through this moment. I release them from any form of guilt and shame, in the name of Jesus Christ. I hereby plead the blood of Jesus over any sins committed by my parents and ancestors. I cancel through the Blood of Jesus Christ, any satanic covenants, exchanges, vows or transactions made over my life, body, soul, spirit, and circumstances, in the name of Jesus Christ. I cancel every legal right that the devil may have against me, by the blood of Jesus Christ. The accuser of the brethren will have nothing against me as I come to the presence of God in prayer.

The devil cannot hinder or delay my prayer, because I know who I am. I am a child of the Kingdom; I am a king and priest of the

Lord, redeemed from the hand of the devil by the blood of Jesus Christ. I declare that all satanic thrones, altars, dominions, principalities, powers, rulers of darkness, queen of the coast, queen of heavens, household wickedness, spiritual hosts of wickedness and all satanic works, have no power or authority over my life. I declare that satanic harassment and intimidation have no effect on me.

Today I receive divine strength to pray; I will not pray in vain. I will not pray amiss. My prayers will bring the desired results. I command the fountain of prayer to open now, and flow into my life, I command the warring angels of God to descend and fight on my behalf. Every minute and every hour that I spend in prayer will bring solution. Every prayer point will attract divine attention and divine intervention. I decree open heavens over my prayers, and today, God of heaven and earth will attend to my case. My prayers today will shake the heavens and move the earth; testimonies, miracles, healing, breakthrough, signs and wonders will follow my prayers. At the end of this prayer session, my life will never be the same again.

PRAYER POINTS:

1. O God my Father, thank you for being my God, my Father and my friend.
2. O God my Father, thank you for the privilege to know you and the power of the resurrection of Jesus Christ.
3. O God my Father, thank you for always being there for me and with me.
4. O God my Father, thank you for the great and mighty things that you are doing in my life.

5. O God my Father, thank you for your provision and protection over me and my household.
6. O God my Father, thank you for always answering my prayers.
7. I confess my sins before you today and I ask you to forgive me on the basis of your mercy, in the name of Jesus Christ.
8. Wash me clean today O Lord by the blood of Jesus Christ.
9. I cover myself and my household with the blood of Jesus Christ.
10. My prayers today will not go in vain; my prayers will produce the desired results in the name of Jesus Christ.
11. Father Lord I have suffered enough from the hands of my enemies, let my days of joy come.
12. Father Lord I have suffered enough from the hands of my household wickedness, let my glory appear by fire.
13. Father Lord I have suffered enough from the hands of the spirit of poverty, let my blessings come right now.
14. Father Lord I have suffered enough from the hands of the spirit of stagnancy, let my life move forward.
15. Father Lord I have suffered enough delay, let my life progress.
16. Father Lord I have suffered enough demotion, let my promotion come by fire Father Lord I have suffered enough from the hands of sickness, let my healing be made perfect.
17. Father Lord I have suffered enough slavery, liberate me by fire.
18. Father Lord I have suffered enough chains and bondage, set me free today.

19. Father Lord I have suffered enough failure, from this moment I shall fail no more.
20. Father Lord I have suffered enough disappointment, from this moment surround me with good people.
21. Father Lord I have suffered enough shame, remove my shame today by your power.
22. Father Lord I have suffered enough pain, heal my pain now.
23. My days of joy shall come by fire.
24. My time of prosperity, come by fire.
25. My hour of deliverance, come now by fire.
26. My days of blessings, come now by fire.
27. My days of miracles, come now by fire.
28. Blood of Jesus, wipe away every mark of poverty.
29. Blood of Jesus, wipe away every mark of sickness.
30. Blood of Jesus, wipe away every mark of sudden death.
31. Blood of Jesus, wipe away every mark of backwardness.
32. Blood of Jesus, wipe away every mark of failure.
33. Blood of Jesus, wipe away every mark of the enemy.
34. Blood of Jesus, wipe away every mark of failure at the edge of miracles.
35. O God my Father, put an end to my pain.
36. O God my Father, put an end to my sickness.
37. O God my Father, put an end to my sorrow.
38. O God my Father, put an end to my failure.
39. O God my Father, put an end to hard labor less blessings in my life.
40. O God my Father, put an end to my crying.
41. O God my Father, put an end to my hopeless situations.
42. O God my Father, put an end to poverty in my life.
43. O God my Father, put an end to sufferings in my life.

I cover my prayers in the blood of Jesus Christ. According to the Word of God, I have asked, I shall receive. I have knocked the door, it shall be opened unto me. I have sought, I shall find, in the name of Jesus Christ. It is written, "… Decree a thing, and it shall be established". As I have spoken in prayer, it shall be so. My prayers shall produce desire results. My prayers shall produce desired miracles. My prayers shall produce desired testimonies, in the name of Jesus Christ. Territorial spirit and power cannot hinder this prayer. Sins and flesh cannot hinder this prayer. It is done. It is sealed by the blood of Jesus Christ. It is delivered to me, in Jesus might name. Amen!

DAY EIGHT

PRAYER TO OVERTURN STUBBORN SITUATIONS

Passages To Read Before You Pray:
Ezekiel 21:27, Isaiah 43:18-19, Psalms 34, 86, 40, 70, Jeremiah 32:36-43, 33:14, 1 John 3:8,

In the book of Job 22:28, the Scripture says when I decree a thing, it shall be established for me. I stand on this Scripture and decree. I have come today to fellowship with my heavenly Father, and make my requests and needs known unto Him. I cannot be hindered nor delayed because I know who I am in the Lord. I am a child of the Kingdom, born of the Spirit, redeemed by the blood of Jesus Christ. I walk in authority, living life without any apology because the power and authority has been given to me according to the Word of God in the book of Luke 9:1.

As I have come to pray today and to fellowship with my heavenly Father, I cover myself in the blood of Jesus Christ, and I put on the whole armor of God. I hereby come against every Prince of Persia that wants to hinder my prayer, I arrest you by the power in the blood of Jesus Christ, and I bind you and cast you down into the pit of hell.

I come against principalities and powers that wrestle with me and my prayers, I arrest you today by the power in the name of Jesus Christ, and I bind you and cast down into the pit of hell. I come against the rulers of the darkness of this world, against spiritual wickedness in high places, I arrest you all by the power in the name of Jesus Christ, and I bind you and cast you down into the pit of hell. I come against weakness and weariness, I arrest you today by the power in the name of Jesus Christ, and I bind you and cast you out of my life. I come against wondering spirit and distractions, I arrest you today by the power in the name of Jesus Christ, and I bind you and cast you out of my life.

Today I receive the anointing to pray and get results, my prayers cannot be hindered nor delayed because Jesus is my Lord, I will pray today and get the desired results, I decree open heavens upon my prayers. I baptize myself in the fire of the Holy Ghost; therefore I have become too hot for the enemy to handle. My prayers today will attract divine intervention to every situation in my life; signs and wonders will follow my prayers today, testimonies will follow my prayers today and the name of God alone will be glorified, in Jesus name. Amen!

PRAYER POINTS:

1. O God my Father, thank you for being my God, my Father and my friend.
2. O God my Father, thank you for the privilege to know you and the power of the resurrection of Jesus Christ.
3. O God my Father, thank you for always being there for me and with me.
4. O God my Father, thank you for the great and mighty things that you are doing in my life.
5. O God my Father, thank you for your provision and protection over me and my household.
6. O God my Father, thank you for always answering my prayers.

7. I confess my sins before you today and I ask you to forgive me on the basis of your mercy, in the name of Jesus Christ.
8. Wash me clean today O Lord by the blood of Jesus Christ.
9. I cover myself and my household with the blood of Jesus Christ.
10. My prayers today will not go in vain; my prayers will produce the desired results in the name of Jesus Christ.
11. O God my Father, let every judgment against me be overturned by your power, in the name of Jesus Christ.
12. O God my Father, it is high time, let every unpleasant situation in my life be overturned by the power, in the name of Jesus Christ.
13. O God my Father, let every satanic decree against me be overturned today, in the name of Jesus Christ.
14. O God my Father, let every satanic decree against my family be overturned today, in the name of Jesus Christ.
15. O God my Father, let every satanic decree against my destiny be overturned today, in the name of Jesus Christ.
16. O God my Father, let every satanic decree against my future be overturned now, in the name of Jesus Christ.
17. O God my Father, let every satanic decree against my children be overturned now, in the name of Jesus Christ.
18. O God my Father, let every satanic decree against my marriage be overturned now, in the name of Jesus Christ.
19. O God my Father, let every satanic decree against my business be overturned now, in the name of Jesus Christ.
20. O God my Father, let every satanic decree against my finances be overturned now, in the name of Jesus Christ.

21. Any decision made anywhere against the plan of God for me, be overturned now by the fire of God, in the name of Jesus Christ.
22. Any decision made anywhere in contrary to the plan of God for my future, be overturned now, by the fire of God in the name of Jesus Christ.
23. Any decision made anywhere in contrary to the divine agenda for my marriage, be overturned now, in the name of Jesus Christ.
24. Any decision made anywhere in contrary to the divine plan for my children, be overturned now by the fire of God, in the name of Jesus Christ.
25. Any decision made anywhere to make my life miserable is overturned by the fire of God, in the name of Jesus Christ.
26. Any decision made anywhere to frustrate my life is overturned now by the fire of God, in the name of Jesus Christ.
27. Any decision made anywhere to make me labor in vain is overturned now, by the power in the name of Jesus Christ.
28. Any decision made anywhere to make my life a living hell, be overturned now, by the power in the name of Jesus Christ.
29. Any decision made anywhere to rob me of my blessings is overturned now, by the authority in the name of Jesus Christ.
30. Any decision made anywhere to rob me of my miracles is overturned now by the authority in the name of Jesus Christ.

31. O God my Father, let every evil pronouncement against my life be overturned now, until it shall be no more, in the name of Jesus Christ.
32. O God my Father, let the spirit and power of poverty that want to take over my life be overturned now, until it shall be no more, in the name of Jesus Christ.
33. O God my Father, let the power of stagnancy over my life be overturned now until it shall be no more, in the name of Jesus Christ.
34. O God my Father, let the situation that makes me cry be overturned and overturned until it shall be no more, in the name of Jesus Christ.
35. O God my Father, let the problem that challenges my faith in you be overturned and overturned until it shall be no more, in the name of Jesus Christ.
36. O God my Father, let inherited failure in my life be overturned and overturned until it shall be no more, in the name of Jesus Christ.
37. O God my Father, let inherited sickness in my life be overturned and overturned until it shall be no more, in the name of Jesus Christ.
38. O God my Father, let every work of the devil in my life be overturned and overturned until it shall be no more, in the name of Jesus Christ.
39. O God my Father, let every power that causes me to make mistake at the edge of breakthrough be overturned and overturned until it shall be no more, in the name of Jesus Christ.
40. O God my Father, let the expectation of the enemy over my life be overturned and overturned until it shall be no more, in the name of Jesus Christ.

41. O God my Father, Let my shame be overturned and overturned today until it shall be no more, in the name of Jesus Christ.
42. O God my Father, let my ridicule be overturned and overturned today until it shall be no more, in the name of Jesus Christ.
43. O God my Father, let inherited curses upon my life be overturned and overturned today until it shall be no more, in the name of Jesus Christ.
44. O God my Father, let the situation that sets limit on my success be overturned and overturned today until it shall be no more, in the name of Jesus Christ.

I cover my prayers in the blood of Jesus Christ. According to the Word of God, I have asked, I shall receive. I have knocked the door, it shall be opened unto me. I have sought, I shall find, in the name of Jesus Christ. It is written, "… Decree a thing, and it shall be established". As I have spoken in prayer, it shall be so. My prayers shall produce desire results. My prayers shall produce desired miracles. My prayers shall produce desired testimonies, in the name of Jesus Christ. Territorial spirit and power cannot hinder this prayer. Sins and flesh cannot hinder this prayer. It is done. It is sealed by the blood of Jesus Christ. It is delivered to me, in Jesus might name. Amen!

DAY NINE

PRAYER TO LIVE ON THE MOUNTAIN TOP

Passages To Read Before You Pray:
Isaiah 40:28-31, James 1:5-6, Isaiah 33:6,
Ephesians 1:16-21, Psalms 19, 24, 42, 29

In the book of Job 22:28, the Scripture says when I decree a thing, it shall be established for me. I stand on this Scripture and decree. I have come into the presence of God today to plead my case. I enter through the gate of praise, into the sanctuary of heaven. I cover myself in the precious blood of Jesus Christ. I baptize myself in the fire of the Holy Ghost. I charge this atmosphere with the fire of God, and I take this neighborhood for the Lord. I arrest every principality and power, territorial spirit, and every throne and kingdom that is not of God. I cast you down and I command you never to lift yourself up against me, because I have the life of God in me.

In the name of Jesus Christ, I confess my sins today, and I ask you O Lord to forgive me on the basis of your mercy. With all my heart, I forgive those who have sinned against me; from the past through this moment. I release them from any form of guilt and shame, in the name of Jesus Christ. I hereby plead the blood of Jesus over any sins committed by my parents and ancestors. I cancel through the Blood of Jesus Christ, any satanic covenants, exchanges, vows or transactions, made over my life, body, soul, spirit, and circumstances, in the name of Jesus Christ. I cancel every legal right that the devil may have against me, by the blood of Jesus Christ. The accuser of the brethren will have nothing against me, as I come to the presence of God in prayer.

The devil cannot hinder or delay my prayer, because I know who I am. I am a child of the Kingdom. I am a king and priest of the Lord, redeemed from the hand of the devil by the blood of Jesus Christ. I walk in power. I walk in miracle. Proverbs 18:21 says, death and life are in the power of my tongue; I command the power in my tongue to manifest now. I command my tongue to become fire, to consume all the powers of darkness in the air, the land, the sea, and beneath the earth. I hereby raise Holy Ghost standard against the prince of the power of the air and all the hosts of darkness in the air. I raise Holy Ghost standard against the queen of the coasts and all the hosts of darkness on the land. I raise Holy Ghost standard against the marine kingdom and all the hosts of darkness in the sea. I raise Holy Ghost standard against the kingdom of hell and all the hosts of darkness beneath the earth. I shoot down all the networks of demons gathering to resist my prayers. I rebuke and bind all the controlling forces of darkness standing against my prayers.

I declare that all satanic thrones, altars, dominions, principalities, powers, rulers of darkness, queens of the coast, queens of heavens, household wickedness, spiritual hosts of wickedness and all satanic works, have no power or authority over my life. I declare that satanic harassment and intimidation have no effect on me.

Today, I receive divine strength to pray; I will not pray in vain. I will not pray amiss. My prayers will bring the desired results. I command the fountain of prayer to open now, and to flow into my life, I command the warring angels of God to descend and fight on my behalf. Every minute and every hour that I spend in prayer, will bring solution. Every prayer point will attract divine attention and divine intervention. I decree open heavens over my

prayers, and today, God of heaven and earth will attend to my case. My prayers today will shake the heavens and move the earth. Testimonies, miracles, healings, breakthroughs, and signs and wonders, will follow my prayers. At the end of this prayer session, my life will never be the same again.

PRAYER POINTS

1. O God my Father, thank you for being my God, my Father and my friend.
2. O God my Father, thank you for the privilege to know you and the power of the resurrection of Jesus Christ.
3. O God my Father, thank you for always being there for me and with me.
4. O God my Father, thank you for the great and mighty things that you are doing in my life.
5. O God my Father, thank you for your provision and protection over me and my household.
6. O God my Father, thank you for always answering my prayers.
7. I confess my sins before you today and I ask you to forgive me on the basis of your mercy, in the name of Jesus Christ.
8. Wash me clean today O Lord by the blood of Jesus Christ.
9. I cover myself and my household with the blood of Jesus Christ.
10. My prayers today will not go in vain; my prayers will produce the desired results in the name of Jesus Christ.
11. I stand on the Word of God. I decree that the wisdom of God be operational in my life, in the name of Jesus

Christ.
12. I stand on the Word of God. I receive the grace to access the divine wisdom bank for the unlimited flow of wisdom through the Word of God, in the name of Jesus Christ.
13. O God my Father, let my eyes discover precious thing and let hidden things be brought to light for me, in the name of Jesus Christ.
14. I stand on the Word of God. I receive grace to operate by the surpassing intelligence of God, in the name of Jesus Christ.
15. I stand on the Word of God. I decree that I receive wisdom to bring stability to every area of my life, in the name of Jesus Christ.
16. I stand on the Word of God. I decree that I receive wisdom to bring stability into my family, in the name of Jesus Christ.
17. I stand on the Word of God. I decree that I receive wisdom to bring stability into my business, in the name of Jesus Christ.
18. I stand on the Word of God. I decree that I receive wisdom to bring stability into my spiritual life, in the name of Jesus Christ.
19. I stand on the Word of God. I decree that I receive wisdom to bring stability into my marriage, in the name of Jesus Christ.
20. I stand on the Word of God. I decree that my life will command unusual grace, favor and attraction, in the name of Jesus Christ.
21. I stand on the Word of God. I decree that my days are preserved by God; with long life, in the name of Jesus Christ.

22. I stand on the Word of God. I decree that my days are preserved by God; with riches and honor, in the name of Jesus Christ.
23. I stand on the Word of God. I receive the anointing to make unpredictable and unprecedented progress in life, in the name of Jesus Christ.
24. I stand on the Word of God. I receive the anointing to overcome stagnation in every area of my life, in the name of Jesus Christ.
25. I stand on the Word of God. I receive the anointing to overcome frustration in every area of my life, in the name of Jesus Christ.
26. I stand on the Word of God. I receive the anointing to overcome hardship in every area of my life, in the name of Jesus Christ.
27. I stand on the Word of God. I receive the anointing to overcome struggle in every area of my life, in the name of Jesus Christ.
28. I stand on the Word of God. I decree that nothing is permitted to stop me. I am confident that I will succeed, in the name of Jesus Christ.
29. I stand on the Word of God. I declare that from this moment onwards, I walk in the grace that unravels mysteries and secrets, in the name of Jesus Christ.
30. I stand on the Word of God. I declare that from this moment onwards, nothing shall be hidden from me, in the name of Jesus Christ.
31. I stand on the Word of God. I declare that from this moment onwards, I will be led by the Holy Spirit, in the name of Jesus Christ.
32. I stand on the Word of God. I declare that from this moment onwards, my decisions will be Spirit directed

and instructed, in the name of Jesus Christ.
33. I stand on the Word of God. I declare that from this moment onwards, my judgment will no longer be after my physical senses, in the name of Jesus Christ.
34. O God my Father, open my spiritual hearing so that I can hear your voice leading me, in the name of Jesus Christ.
35. By the power and authority in the name of Jesus Christ, I am no longer subject to the power of deception, in the name of Jesus Christ.
36. By the power and authority in the name of Jesus Christ, I am no longer subject to the power of satanic manipulation, in the name of Jesus Christ.
37. By the power and authority in the name of Jesus Christ, I am no longer subject to demonic mind control, in the name of Jesus Christ.
38. By the power and authority in the name of Jesus Christ, I am no longer subject to the power of evil controllers, in the name of Jesus Christ.
39. By the power and authority in the name of Jesus Christ, I am no longer subject to satanic remote control, in the name of Jesus Christ.
40. O God my Father, let the Holy Spirit guide me in every way I go and every path I take, in the name of Jesus Christ.
41. O God my Father, let the Holy Spirit guide me in every judgment or decision that I make, in the name of Jesus Christ.
42. O God my Father, let the Holy Spirit guide me in making choices as I relate to people, in the name of Jesus Christ.
43. O God my Father, grant me insight and depth of understanding in every area of life, in the name of Jesus

Christ.
44. I stand on the Word of God. I receive grace to operate in a higher and deeper dimension on understanding, in the name of Jesus Christ.
45. O God my Father, grant me revelation of my peculiarities and uniqueness that I may know what you have deposited in me, in the name of Jesus Christ.
46. I stand on the Word of God. I receive grace to understand my purpose. I will not be a waste of God's breath, in the name of Jesus Christ.
47. I stand on the Word of God. I receive grace to understand my calling. I will not be a waste of God's breath, in the name of Jesus Christ.
48. I stand on the Word of God. I receive grace to understand God's plans for my life. I will not be a waste of God's breath, in the name of Jesus Christ.
49. O God my Father, let my eyes of understanding open according to your Word, in the name of Jesus Christ.
50. I stand on the Word of God. I decree that the capacity for amazing sight is being developed in me. God is at work in me, in the name of Jesus Christ.
51. I stand on the Word of God. I receive the grace to see the doings of God in me, in the name of Jesus Christ.
52. I stand on the Word of God. I receive the grace to see the doings of God in my marriage, in the name of Jesus Christ.
53. I stand on the Word of God. I receive the grace to see the doings of God in my family, in the name of Jesus Christ.
54. I stand on the Word of God. I receive the grace to see the doings of God in my finances, in the name of Jesus Christ.
55. I stand on the Word of God. I receive the grace to see the

doings of God in my business, in the name of Jesus Christ.
56. I stand on the Word of God. I receive the grace to see the doings of God in my ministry, in the name of Jesus Christ.
57. I stand on the Word of God. I receive the grace to see the doings of God in my home, in the name of Jesus Christ.
58. I stand on the Word of God. I receive the grace to see the doings of God in the life of my spouse, in the name of Jesus Christ.
59. I stand on the Word of God. I receive the grace to see the doings of God in my children, in the name of Jesus Christ.
60. I stand on the Word of God. I receive the grace to see the doings of God all around me, in the name of Jesus Christ.

I cover my prayers in the blood of Jesus Christ. According to the Word of God, I have asked; I shall receive. I have knocked the door; it shall be opened unto me. I have sought; I shall find, in the name of Jesus Christ. It is written, "… Decree a thing, and it shall be established". As I have spoken in prayer, it shall be so. My prayers shall produce desired results. My prayers shall produce desired miracles. My prayers shall produce desired testimonies, in the name of Jesus Christ. Territorial spirit and power cannot hinder this prayer. Sins and flesh cannot hinder this prayer. It is done. It is sealed by the blood of Jesus Christ. It is delivered to me, in Jesus mighty name. Amen!

DAY TEN

I DISAGREE WITH MY ENEMIES

Passages To Read Before You Pray:
Amos 3:3, Isaiah 1:31, Ezekiel 37:1-11, Isaiah 49:24-26, Psalms 97, 35, 3, 83, 9

In the book of Job 22:28, the Scripture says when I decree a thing, it shall be established for me. I stand on this Scripture and decree. I have come into the presence of God today to plead my case. I enter through the gate of praise into the sanctuary of heaven. I cover myself in the precious blood of Jesus Christ. I baptize myself in the fire of the Holy Ghost. I charge this atmosphere with the fire of God, and I take this neighborhood for the Lord. I arrest every principality and power, territorial spirit, and every throne and kingdom that is not of God. I cast you down and I command you never to lift yourself up against me, because I have the life of God in me.

In the name of Jesus Christ, I confess my sins today, and I ask you O Lord to forgive me on the basis of your mercy. With all my heart, I forgive those who have sinned against me from the past through this moment. I release them from any form of guilt and shame, in the name of Jesus Christ. I hereby plead the blood of Jesus over any sins committed by my parents and ancestors. I cancel through the Blood of Jesus Christ, any satanic covenants, exchanges, vows or transactions made over my life, body, soul, spirit, and circumstances, in the name of Jesus Christ. I cancel every legal right that the devil may have against me, by the blood of Jesus Christ. The accuser of the brethren will have nothing against me as I come to the presence of God in prayer.

The devil cannot hinder or delay my prayer, because I know who I am. I am a child of the Kingdom; I am a king and priest of the Lord, redeemed from the hand of the devil by the blood of Jesus Christ. I declare that all satanic thrones, altars, dominions, principalities, powers, rulers of darkness, queen of the coast, queen of heavens, household wickedness, spiritual hosts of wickedness and all satanic works, have no power or authority over my life. I declare that satanic harassment and intimidation have no effect on me.

Today I receive divine strength to pray; I will not pray in vain. I will not pray amiss. My prayers will bring the desired results. I command the fountain of prayer to open now, and flow into my life, I command the warring angels of God to descend and fight on my behalf. Every minute and every hour that I spend in prayer will bring solution. Every prayer point will attract divine attention and divine intervention. I decree open heavens over my prayers, and today, God of heaven and earth will attend to my case. My prayers today will shake the heavens and move the earth; testimonies, miracles, healing, breakthrough, signs and wonders will follow my prayers. At the end of this prayer session, my life will never be the same again.

PRAYER POINTS

1. O God my Father, thank you for being my God, my Father and my friend.
2. O God my Father, thank you for the privilege to know you and the power of the resurrection of Jesus Christ.
3. O God my Father, thank you for always being there for me and with me.

4. O God my Father, thank you for the great and mighty things that you are doing in my life.
5. O God my Father, thank you for your provision and protection over me and my household.
6. O God my Father, thank you for always answering my prayers.
7. I confess my sins before you today and I ask you to forgive me on the basis of your mercy, in the name of Jesus Christ.
8. Wash me clean today O Lord by the blood of Jesus Christ.
9. I cover myself and my household with the blood of Jesus Christ.
10. My prayers today will not go in vain; my prayers will produce the desired results in the name of Jesus Christ.
11. I disagree with the work of the devil going on in my life, in the name of Jesus Christ.
12. I disagree with the work of the devil going on in my marriage, in the name of Jesus Christ.
13. I disagree with the work of the devil going on concerning my health, in the name of Jesus Christ.
14. I disagree with the work of the devil going on in my finances, in the name of Jesus Christ.
15. I disagree with the work of the devil going on in the lives of my children, in the name of Jesus Christ.
16. I disagree with the work of the devil going on in the life of my spouse, in the name of Jesus Christ.
17. I disagree with the work of the devil going on in my family, in the name of Jesus Christ.
18. I disagree with the work of the devil going on in my workplace, in the name of Jesus Christ.

19. I disagree with the work of the devil going on in my business, in the name of Jesus Christ.
20. I disagree with the work of the devil going on concerning my destiny, in the name of Jesus Christ.
21. I disagree with everything that the enemy is doing in my life; enough is enough, in the name of Jesus Christ.
22. Any power anywhere assigned to work against me, I refuse to allow you to destroy my life, in the name of Jesus Christ.
23. Any power anywhere assigned to work against me, I refuse to allow you to destroy my marriage, in the name of Jesus Christ.
24. Any power anywhere assigned to work against me, I refuse to allow you to destroy what God is doing in my life, in the name of Jesus Christ.
25. Any power anywhere assigned to work against me, I refuse to allow you to control my life, in the name of Jesus Christ.
26. Any power anywhere assigned to work against me, I refuse to allow you to hold my life back, in the name of Jesus Christ.
27. Any power anywhere assigned to work against me, I refuse to allow you to stop what God is doing in my life, in the name of Jesus Christ.
28. Any power anywhere assigned to work against me, I refuse to allow you to stop my progress, in the name of Jesus Christ.
29. Any power anywhere assigned to work against me, I refuse to allow you to hinder my prayer, in the name of Jesus Christ.

30. Any power anywhere assigned to work against me, I refuse to allow you to delay my miracles, in the name of Jesus Christ.
31. Any power anywhere assigned to work against me, I refuse to allow you to block my blessings, in the name of Jesus Christ.
32. Any power anywhere assigned to work against me, I refuse to allow you to delay my financial breakthrough, in the name of Jesus Christ.
33. By the power and authority in the blood of Jesus Christ, I block every access to my life that I have ignorantly given to the enemy, in the name of Jesus Christ.
34. By the power and authority in the blood of Jesus Christ, I block every access to my finances that I have ignorantly given to the enemy, in the name of Jesus Christ.
35. By the power and authority in the blood of Jesus Christ, I block every access to my family affairs that I have ignorantly given to the enemy, in the name of Jesus Christ.
36. By the power and authority in the blood of Jesus Christ, I block every access to my marital success that I have ignorantly given to the enemy, in the name of Jesus Christ.
37. I release the fire of God to destroy every roadblock that I have ignorantly set up against myself, in the name of Jesus Christ.
38. I release the fire of God to destroy every roadblock that I have ignorantly set up against my breakthroughs, in the name of Jesus Christ.

39. I release the fire of God to destroy every roadblock that I have ignorantly setup against my miracles, in the name of Jesus Christ.
40. I release the fire of God to destroy every roadblock that I have ignorantly set up against my blessings, in the name of Jesus Christ.
41. I release the fire of God to destroy every roadblock that I have ignorantly set up against my marriage, in the name of Jesus Christ.
42. I release the fire of God to destroy every roadblock that I have ignorantly set up against my spiritual growth, in the name of Jesus Christ.
43. I release the fire of God to destroy every roadblock that I have ignorantly set up against my divine helpers, in the name of Jesus Christ.
44. I release the fire of God to destroy every roadblock that I have ignorantly set up against my prayers, in the name of Jesus Christ.
45. I release the fire of God to destroy every roadblock that I have ignorantly set up against my financial miracles, in the name of Jesus Christ.
46. I release the fire of God to destroy every roadblock that I have ignorantly set up against my divine opportunities, in the name of Jesus Christ.
47. I release the fire of God to destroy every altar of wickedness built against me, in the name of Jesus Christ.
48. I release the fire of God to destroy every altar of wickedness built against my family, in the name of Jesus Christ.
49. I release the fire of God to destroy every altar of wickedness built against my spouse in the name of Jesus Christ.

50. I release the fire of God to destroy every altar of wickedness built against my children, in the name of Jesus Christ.
51. I release the fire of God to destroy every altar of wickedness built against my marriage, in the name of Jesus Christ.
52. I release the fire of God to destroy every altar of wickedness built against my prayer altar, in the name of Jesus Christ.
53. I release the fire of God to destroy every altar of wickedness built against my purpose and destiny, in the name of Jesus Christ.
54. I release the fire of God to destroy every altar of wickedness built against my dreams and future, in the name of Jesus Christ.
55. Any power anywhere forcing me to pay what I did not owe, you will not escape the judgment of God, in the name of Jesus Christ.
56. Any power anywhere forcing me to operate outside the will of God for me, you will not escape the judgment of God, in the name of Jesus Christ.
57. My life is not a chess board. I command the devil to stop playing games with my life, in the name of Jesus Christ.
58. My life is not a chess board. I command household wickedness to stop playing games with my life, in the name of Jesus Christ.
59. My life is not a chess board. I command principalities and powers to stop playing games with my life, in the name of Jesus Christ.
60. By the power in the name of Jesus Christ, I come against every satanic go slow in my life.

61. By the power in the name of Jesus Christ, I come against every satanic go slow in my marriage.
62. By the power in the name of Jesus Christ, I come against every satanic go slow in my finances.
63. By the power in the name of Jesus Christ, I come against every satanic go slow in my business.
64. By the power in the name of Jesus Christ, I come against every satanic go slow in my ministry.
65. By the power in the name of Jesus Christ, I come against every satanic go slow in every area of my life.
66. By the power and authority in the name of Jesus Christ, I am coming out of my problems today.
67. By the power and authority in the name of Jesus Christ, I am coming out of my stubborn situations today.
68. By the power and authority in the name of Jesus Christ, I am coming out of Egyptian slavery today.
69. By the power and authority in the name of Jesus Christ, I am coming out of Egyptian bondage today.
70. By the power and authority in the name of Jesus Christ, I am coming out of my hopeless situations today.
71. By the power and authority in the name of Jesus Christ, I am coming out of any form of sickness and infirmity today.
72. By the power and authority in the name of Jesus Christ, I am coming out of the bondage of poverty today.
73. By the power and authority in the name of Jesus Christ, I am coming out of the bondage of failure today.
74. By the power and authority in the name of Jesus Christ, I am coming out of the bondage of backwardness today.
75. By the power and authority in the name of Jesus Christ, I am coming out of the bondage of stagnancy today.

76. By the power and authority in the name of Jesus Christ, I am coming out of evil cycle in my life today.
77. By the power and authority in the name of Jesus Christ, I am coming out of long time problems in my life today.
78. By the power and authority in the name of Jesus Christ, I am coming out of debts today.
79. By the power and authority in the name of Jesus Christ, I am coming out of the bondage of household wickedness today.
80. By the power and authority in the name of Jesus Christ, I am coming out of the bondage of witchcraft today.
81. By the power and authority in the name of Jesus Christ, I am coming out of fruitless hard labor today.
82. By the power and authority in the name of Jesus Christ, I am coming out of season of tears in my life and I enter into season of rejoicing.
83. By the power and authority in the name of Jesus Christ, I am coming out of collective captivity in every area of my life today.
84. By the power and authority in the name of Jesus Christ, I am coming out of satanic cage holding my life back.
85. By the power and authority in the name of Jesus Christ, I am coming out of any form of depression.
86. By the power and authority in the name of Jesus Christ, I am coming out of any form of satanic oppression.
87. O God my Father, let every traffic light of my life turn green. I am ready to move forward, in the name of Jesus Christ.
88. O God my Father, let every traffic light of my life turn green. I refuse to be delayed, in the name of Jesus Christ.

89. O God my Father, let every traffic light of my life turn green. I am ready to fulfill purpose and destiny, in the name of Jesus Christ.
90. I command every dry and scattered bone of my life to receive the life of God and come together now, in the name of Jesus Christ.
91. I command every dry and scattered bone of my destiny to receive the life of God and come together now, in the name of Jesus Christ.
92. I command every dry and scattered bone of my marriage to receive the life of God and come together now, in the name of Jesus Christ.
93. I command every dry and scattered bone of my business to receive the life of God and come together now, in the name of Jesus Christ.
94. I refuse to be a victim of satanic attacks, in the name of Jesus Christ.
95. I refuse to be a subject of satanic experiment, in the name of Jesus Christ.
96. By the power and authority in the name of Jesus Christ, I cancel every witchcraft operation in every area of my life.
97. By the power and authority in the blood of Jesus Christ, I overcome every opposition against the plan of God for my life, in the name of Jesus Christ.
98. Any power anywhere trying to turn my life into a war zone, you will not escape the judgment of God, in the name of Jesus Christ.
99. Any power anywhere trying to turn my marriage into a war zone, you will not escape the judgment of God, in the name of Jesus Christ.

100. Any power anywhere trying to turn my home into a battlefield, you will not escape the judgment of God, in the name of Jesus Christ.

I cover my prayers in the blood of Jesus Christ. According to the Word of God, I have asked, I shall receive. I have knocked the door, it shall be opened unto me. I have sought, I shall find, in the name of Jesus Christ. It is written, "... Decree a thing, and it shall be established". As I have spoken in prayer, it shall be so. My prayers shall produce desire results. My prayers shall produce desired miracles. My prayers shall produce desired testimonies, in the name of Jesus Christ. Territorial spirit and power cannot hinder this prayer. Sins and flesh cannot hinder this prayer. It is done. It is sealed by the blood of Jesus Christ. It is delivered to me, in Jesus might name. Amen!

DAY ELEVEN

PRAYER TO FIGHT & CONQUER

Passages To Read Before You Pray:
Matthew 16:18-19, Luke 10:19, Jeremiah 1:8, 19, Psalms 3, 35, 68, 17, 83

In the book of Job 22:28, the Scripture says when I decree a thing, it shall be established for me. I stand on this Scripture and decree. I have come into the presence of God today to plead my case. I enter through the gate of praise, into the sanctuary of heaven. I cover myself in the precious blood of Jesus Christ. I baptize myself in the fire of the Holy Ghost. I charge this atmosphere with the fire of God, and I take this neighborhood for the Lord. I arrest every principality and power, territorial spirit, and every throne and kingdom that is not of God. I cast you down and I command you never to lift yourself up against me, because I have the life of God in me.

In the name of Jesus Christ, I confess my sins today, and I ask you O Lord to forgive me on the basis of your mercy. With all my heart, I forgive those who have sinned against me; from the past through this moment. I release them from any form of guilt and shame, in the name of Jesus Christ. I hereby plead the blood of Jesus over any sins committed by my parents and ancestors. I cancel through the Blood of Jesus Christ, any satanic covenants, exchanges, vows or transactions, made over my life, body, soul, spirit, and circumstances, in the name of Jesus Christ. I cancel every legal right that the devil may have against me, by the blood of Jesus Christ. The accuser of the brethren will have nothing against me, as I come to the presence of God in prayer.

The devil cannot hinder or delay my prayer, because I know who I am. I am a child of the Kingdom. I am a king and priest of the Lord, redeemed from the hand of the devil by the blood of Jesus Christ. I walk in power. I walk in miracle. Proverbs 18:21 says, death and life are in the power of my tongue; I command the power in my tongue to manifest now. I command my tongue to become fire, to consume all the powers of darkness in the air, the land, the sea, and beneath the earth. I hereby raise Holy Ghost standard against the prince of the power of the air and all the hosts of darkness in the air. I raise Holy Ghost standard against the queen of the coasts and all the hosts of darkness on the land. I raise Holy Ghost standard against the marine kingdom and all the hosts of darkness in the sea. I raise Holy Ghost standard against the kingdom of hell and all the hosts of darkness beneath the earth. I shoot down all the networks of demons gathering to resist my prayers. I rebuke and bind all the controlling forces of darkness standing against my prayers.

I declare that all satanic thrones, altars, dominions, principalities, powers, rulers of darkness, queens of the coast, queens of heavens, household wickedness, spiritual hosts of wickedness and all satanic works, have no power or authority over my life. I declare that satanic harassment and intimidation have no effect on me.

Today, I receive divine strength to pray; I will not pray in vain. I will not pray amiss. My prayers will bring the desired results. I command the fountain of prayer to open now, and to flow into my life, I command the warring angels of God to descend and fight on my behalf. Every minute and every hour that I spend in prayer, will bring solution. Every prayer point will attract divine attention and divine intervention. I decree open heavens over my

prayers, and today, God of heaven and earth will attend to my case. My prayers today will shake the heavens and move the earth. Testimonies, miracles, healings, breakthroughs, and signs and wonders, will follow my prayers. At the end of this prayer session, my life will never be the same again.

PRAYER POINTS

1. O God my Father, thank you for being my God, my Father and my friend.
2. O God my Father, thank you for the privilege to know you and the power of the resurrection of Jesus Christ.
3. O God my Father, thank you for always being there for me and with me.
4. O God my Father, thank you for the great and mighty things that you are doing in my life.
5. O God my Father, thank you for your provision and protection over me and my household.
6. O God my Father, thank you for always answering my prayers.
7. I confess my sins before you today and I ask you to forgive me on the basis of your mercy, in the name of Jesus Christ.
8. Wash me clean today O Lord by the blood of Jesus Christ.
9. I cover myself and my household with the blood of Jesus Christ.
10. My prayers today will not go in vain; my prayers will produce the desired results in the name of Jesus Christ.
11. O God my Father, arise and march forth like a might Hero; fight and destroy the power of the enemy that

wants me to die without fulfilling purpose, in the name of Jesus Christ.
12. O God my Father, arise and come out like a warrior; fight against household wickedness trying to hinder what you are doing in my life, in the name of Jesus Christ.
13. O God my Father, arise in your anger; crush any power anywhere squandering the blessing that you have prepared for me, in the name of Jesus Christ. *Isaiah 42:13*.
14. By the authority and power in the blood of Jesus Christ, I advance and possess the territory of my enemy, in the name of Jesus Christ.
15. By the authority and power in the blood of Jesus Christ, I advance and possess the gates of my enemy, in the name of Jesus Christ.
16. By the authority and power in the blood of Jesus Christ, I advance and take over the source of my enemy's power, in the name of Jesus Christ.
17. By the authority and power in the blood of Jesus Christ, I advance and take over the source of my enemy's provision, in the name of Jesus Christ.
18. By the authority and power in the blood of Jesus Christ, I advance and take over the source of my enemy's strength, in the name of Jesus Christ.
19. By the authority and power in the blood of Jesus Christ, I advance and possess the land flowing with milk and honey, in the name of Jesus Christ.
20. By the authority and power in the blood of Jesus Christ, I advance and possess my promise land, in the name of Jesus Christ.
21. I stand on the Word of God. I walk around the city and possess the land God has planned for me, in the name of

Jesus Christ.

22. I stand on the Word of God. I walk around the property and possess the house God has planned for me, in the name of Jesus Christ.
23. I stand on the Word of God. I walk around the property and possess the house God has planned for my family, in the name of Jesus Christ.
24. I stand on the Word of God. I walk around the property and possess the car God has planned for me, in the name of Jesus Christ.
25. I stand on the Word of God. I walk around the property and possess everything God has planned for me, in the name of Jesus Christ.
26. I stand on the Word of God. I command afflictions in my life to end now, in the name of Jesus Christ.
27. I stand on the Word of God. I command troubles in my life to end now, in the name of Jesus Christ.
28. I stand on the Word of God. I command frustration in my life to end now, in the name of Jesus Christ.
29. I stand on the Word of God. I command spiritual battles in my life to end now, in the name of Jesus Christ.
30. I stand on the Word of God. I command financial struggles in my life to end now, in the name of Jesus Christ.
31. I stand on the Word of God. I command marital struggles in my life to end now, in the name of Jesus Christ.
32. I stand on the Word of God. I command employment struggles in my life to end now, in the name of Jesus Christ.
33. O God my Father, let my battle cry provoke divine intervention, in the name of Jesus Christ.

34. O God my Father, let my battle cry provoke angelic assistance, in the name of Jesus Christ.
35. O God my Father, let my battle cry provoke the hosts of heaven to arise and fight for me, in the name of Jesus Christ.
36. O God my Father, let my battle cry provoke the hosts of heaven to arise and rescue me from the hands of Pharaoh, in the name of Jesus Christ.
37. O God my Father, let my battle cry provoke the hosts of heaven to arise and rescue me from the power of the Egyptians that want to enslave me, in the name of Jesus Christ.
38. O God my Father, let my battle cry provoke the hosts of heaven to arise and fight against my household wickedness, in the name of Jesus Christ.
39. O God my Father, let my battle cry provoke the hosts of heaven to arise and fight against the power of my father's house, in the name of Jesus Christ.
40. Jehovah, you are my Father and my God; arise today and take me to a better place of fulfillment, in the name of Jesus Christ.
41. Jehovah, you are my Father and my God; arise today and take my family to a better place, in the name of Jesus Christ.
42. Jehovah, you are my Father and my God; arise today and take my marriage to a better place, in the name of Jesus Christ.
43. Jehovah, you are my Father and my God; arise today and take my career to a better place, in the name of Jesus Christ.
44. Jehovah, you are my Father and my God; arise today and take my health to a better place, in the name of Jesus

Christ.

45. Jehovah, you are my Father and my God; arise today and take my business to a better place, in the name of Jesus Christ.
46. Jehovah, you are my Father and my God; arise today and take my destiny to a better place, in the name of Jesus Christ.
47. O God my Father, you are the King of Glory; beat every enemy of my life and destiny into submission like you did to Pharaoh, in the name of Jesus Christ.
48. O God my Father, slow down my adversaries, and destroy their works. Their hands will not be able to fulfill their enterprise towards me, in the name of Jesus Christ.
49. O God my Father, slow down my adversaries, and destroy their works. Their hands will not be able to fulfill their enterprise towards my family, in the name of Jesus Christ.
50. O God my Father, slow down my adversaries, and destroy their works. Their hands will not be able to fulfill their enterprise towards my marriage, in the name of Jesus Christ.
51. O God my Father, slow down my adversaries, and destroy their works. Their hands will not be able to fulfill their enterprise towards my spouse, in the name of Jesus Christ.
52. O God my Father, slow down my adversaries, and destroy their works. Their hands will not be able to fulfill their enterprise towards my children, in the name of Jesus Christ.
53. O God my Father, slow down my adversaries, and destroy their works. Their hands will not be able to

fulfill their enterprise concerning my finances, in the name of Jesus Christ.

I cover my prayers in the blood of Jesus Christ. According to the Word of God, I have asked; I shall receive. I have knocked the door; it shall be opened unto me. I have sought; I shall find, in the name of Jesus Christ. It is written, "… Decree a thing, and it shall be established". As I have spoken in prayer, it shall be so. My prayers shall produce desired results. My prayers shall produce desired miracles. My prayers shall produce desired testimonies, in the name of Jesus Christ. Territorial spirit and power cannot hinder this prayer. Sins and flesh cannot hinder this prayer. It is done. It is sealed by the blood of Jesus Christ. It is delivered to me, in Jesus mighty name. Amen!

DAY TWELVE

PRAYER FOR GOD TO SHOWCASE HIS POWER

Passages To Read Before You Pray:
Isaiah 43:18-19, 2 Kings 2:1-18, John 11:1-48,
Psalms 46, 19, 126

In the book of Job 22:28, the Scripture says when I decree a thing, it shall be established for me. I stand on this Scripture and decree. I have come today to fellowship with my heavenly Father, and make my requests and needs known unto Him. I cannot be hindered nor delayed because I know who I am in the Lord. I am a child of the Kingdom, born of the Spirit, redeemed by the blood of Jesus Christ. I walk in authority, living life without any apology because the power and authority has been given to me according to the Word of God in the book of Luke 9:1.

As I have come to pray today and to fellowship with my heavenly Father, I cover myself in the blood of Jesus Christ, and I put on the whole armor of God. I hereby come against every Prince of Persia that wants to hinder my prayer, I arrest you by the power in the blood of Jesus Christ, and I bind you and cast you down into the pit of hell.

I come against principalities and powers that wrestle with me and my prayers, I arrest you today by the power in the name of Jesus Christ, and I bind you and cast down into the pit of hell. I come against the rulers of the darkness of this world, against spiritual wickedness in high places, I arrest you all by the power in the name of Jesus Christ, and I bind you and cast you down into the pit of hell. I come against weakness and weariness, I arrest you today by the power in the name of Jesus Christ, and I bind you and cast you out of my life. I come against wondering spirit and distractions, I arrest you today by the power in the name of Jesus Christ, and I bind you and cast you out of my life.

Today I receive the anointing to pray and get results, my prayers cannot be hindered nor delayed because Jesus is my Lord, I will pray today and get the desired results, I decree open heavens upon my prayers. I baptize myself in the fire of the Holy Ghost; therefore I have become too hot for the enemy to handle. My prayers today will attract divine intervention to every situation in my life; signs and wonders will follow my prayers today, testimonies will follow my prayers today and the name of God alone will be glorified, in Jesus name. Amen!

PRAYER POINTS

1. O God my Father, thank you for being my God, my Father and my friend.
2. O God my Father, thank you for the privilege to know you and the power of the resurrection of Jesus Christ.
3. O God my Father, thank you for always being there for me and with me.
4. O God my Father, thank you for the great and mighty things that you are doing in my life.
5. O God my Father, thank you for your provision and protection over me and my household.
6. O God my Father, thank you for always answering my prayers.

7. I confess my sins before you today and I ask you to forgive me on the basis of your mercy, in the name of Jesus Christ.
8. Wash me clean today O Lord by the blood of Jesus Christ.
9. I cover myself and my household with the blood of Jesus Christ.
10. My prayers today will not go in vain; my prayers will produce the desired results in the name of Jesus Christ.
11. In the presence of those who are waiting to mock me, O God my Father, demonstrate your power that they may know that you are my God, in the name of Jesus Christ.
12. In the presence of those who are waiting to celebrate my failure, O God my Father, grant me an immeasurable success that they may know you are my God, in the name of Jesus Christ.
13. In the presence of those who are waiting to see what will become of me, O God my Father, demonstrate your power that they may know you are my God, in the name of Jesus Christ.
14. In the presence of those who are waiting to mock the outcome of my prayers, O God my Father, answer my prayer by fire that they may know you are my God, in the name of Jesus Christ.
15. O God my Father, in the presence of those who are waiting to see what you can do for me, demonstrate your power that they may know that you can do all things, in the name of Jesus Christ.
16. O God my Father, in the presence of those who are waiting to see me fall, demonstrate your power that they may know that you are my God, in the name of Jesus Christ.

17. O God my Father, in the presence of those who are waiting to point evil fingers at me, demonstrate your power that they may know you are my God, in the name of Jesus Christ.
18. My helpers, wherever you are, I command you to come forth, in the name of Jesus Christ.
19. My glory, wherever you are, I command you to come forth, in the name of Jesus Christ.
20. My financial freedom, wherever you are, I command you to come forth, in the name of Jesus Christ.
21. My miracles, wherever you are, I command you to come forth, in the name of Jesus Christ.
22. My blessings, wherever you are, I command you to come forth, in the name of Jesus Christ.
23. My financial breakthrough, wherever you are, I command you to come forth, in the name of Jesus Christ.
24. My success, wherever you are, I command you to come forth, in the name of Jesus Christ.
25. People that will show me the way, wherever you are, I command you to come forth, in the name of Jesus Christ.
26. People that will lead me to the top, wherever you are, I command you to come forth, in the name of Jesus Christ.
27. People that God sent to support me, wherever you are, I command you to come forth, in the name of Jesus Christ.
28. People that will show me how to make it, wherever you are, I command you to come forth, in the name of Jesus Christ.
29. People that will contribute to my success, wherever you are, I command you to come forth, in the name of Jesus Christ.

30. People that will show me how to get to the next level, wherever you are, I command you to come forth, in the name of Jesus Christ.
31. People that will connect me to those that will help me, wherever you are, I command you to come forth, in the name of Jesus Christ.
32. O God my Father, I am tired of being the same, let transformation begin to happen in every area of my life, in the name of Jesus Christ.
33. O God my Father, I am tired of being the same, let the new things begin to happen in every area of my life, in the name of Jesus Christ.
34. O God my Father, I am tired of being the same, begin to showcase your power in my life, in the name of Jesus Christ.
35. O God my Father, I am tired of being the same, let extraordinary things begin to happen in my life, in the name of Jesus Christ.
36. O God my Father, I am tired of being the same, let there be supernatural breakthrough in every area of my life, in the name of Jesus Christ.
37. O God my Father, I am tired of being the same, take me from where I am to where you want me to be, in the name of Jesus Christ.
38. O God my Father, I am tired of being the same, catapult me into greatness, in the name of Jesus Christ.
39. O God my Father, I am tired of being the same, catapult me into double promotion, in the name of Jesus Christ.
40. O God my Father, I am tired of being the same, take me to the next level of your power, in the name of Jesus Christ.

41. O God my Father, I am tired of being the same, take me to the next level of your glory, in the name of Jesus Christ.
42. O God my Father, I am tired of being the same, take me to the next level of prosperity, in the name of Jesus Christ.
43. O God my Father, I am tired of being the same, take me to the place of fulfillment, in the name of Jesus Christ.
44. O God my Father, I am tired of being the same, take me to the land that is flowing with milk and honey, in the name of Jesus Christ.
45. O God my Father, I am tired of being the same, transfer me from the valley to the mountain top, in the name of Jesus Christ.
46. O God my Father, I am tired of being the same, let the great and mighty things that you promise begin to happen in my life, in the name of Jesus Christ.
47. O God my Father, I am tired of being the same, give me reasons to sing a new song, in the name of Jesus Christ.
48. O God my Father, I am tired of being the same, give me reasons to dance a new dance, in the name of Jesus Christ.
49. O God my Father, I am tired of being the same, let your power bring the best out of me, in the name of Jesus Christ.
50. O God my Father, I'm tired of being the same, give me reasons to laugh a new laugh, in the name of Jesus Christ.

I cover my prayers in the blood of Jesus Christ. According to the Word of God, I have asked, I shall receive. I have knocked the door, it shall be opened unto me. I have sought, I shall find, in the name of Jesus Christ. It is written, "... Decree a thing, and it shall be established". As I have spoken in prayer, it shall be so. My prayers shall produce desire results. My prayers shall produce desired miracles. My prayers shall produce desired testimonies, in the name of Jesus Christ. Territorial spirit and power cannot hinder this prayer. Sins and flesh cannot hinder this prayer. It is done. It is sealed by the blood of Jesus Christ. It is delivered to me, in Jesus might name. Amen!

DAY THIRTEEN

WAR AGAINST MANIPULATING SPIRIT

Passages To Read Before You Pray:
Genesis 3:1-8, 2 Corinthians 2:11; 11:14, Matthew 4:1-11

In the book of Job 22:28, the Scripture says when I decree a thing, it shall be established for me. I stand on this Scripture and decree. I have come into the presence of God today to plead my case. I enter through the gate of praise into the sanctuary of heaven. I cover myself in the precious blood of Jesus Christ. I baptize myself in the fire of the Holy Ghost. I charge this atmosphere with the fire of God, and I take this neighborhood for the Lord. I arrest every principality and power, territorial spirit, and every throne and kingdom that is not of God. I cast you down and I command you never to lift yourself up against me, because I have the life of God in me.

In the name of Jesus Christ, I confess my sins today, and I ask you O Lord to forgive me on the basis of your mercy. With all my heart, I forgive those who have sinned against me from the past through this moment. I release them from any form of guilt and shame, in the name of Jesus Christ. I hereby plead the blood of Jesus over any sins committed by my parents and ancestors. I cancel through the Blood of Jesus Christ, any satanic covenants, exchanges, vows or transactions made over my life, body, soul, spirit, and circumstances, in the name of Jesus Christ. I cancel every legal right that the devil may have against me, by the blood of Jesus Christ. The accuser of the brethren will have nothing against me as I come to the presence of God in prayer.

The devil cannot hinder or delay my prayer, because I know who I am. I am a child of the Kingdom; I am a king and priest of the

Lord, redeemed from the hand of the devil by the blood of Jesus Christ. I declare that all satanic thrones, altars, dominions, principalities, powers, rulers of darkness, queen of the coast, queen of heavens, household wickedness, spiritual hosts of wickedness and all satanic works, have no power or authority over my life. I declare that satanic harassment and intimidation have no effect on me.

Today I receive divine strength to pray; I will not pray in vain. I will not pray amiss. My prayers will bring the desired results. I command the fountain of prayer to open now, and flow into my life, I command the warring angels of God to descend and fight on my behalf. Every minute and every hour that I spend in prayer will bring solution. Every prayer point will attract divine attention and divine intervention. I decree open heavens over my prayers, and today, God of heaven and earth will attend to my case. My prayers today will shake the heavens and move the earth; testimonies, miracles, healing, breakthrough, signs and wonders will follow my prayers. At the end of this prayer session, my life will never be the same again.

PRAYER POINTS

1. O God my Father, thank you for being my God, my Father and my friend.
2. O God my Father, thank you for the privilege to know you and the power of the resurrection of Jesus Christ.
3. O God my Father, thank you for always being there for me and with me.
4. O God my Father, thank you for the great and mighty things that you are doing in my life.

5. O God my Father, thank you for your provision and protection over me and my household.
6. O God my Father, thank you for always answering my prayers.
7. I confess my sins before you today and I ask you to forgive me on the basis of your mercy, in the name of Jesus Christ.
8. Wash me clean today O Lord by the blood of Jesus Christ.
9. I cover myself and my household with the blood of Jesus Christ.
10. My prayers today will not go in vain; my prayers will produce the desired results in the name of Jesus Christ.
11. Father Lord, I thank you for who you are in my life.
12. I cover myself and my household in the precious blood of Jesus
13. O God my Father, forgive me of all my past mistakes and iniquities.
14. Every manipulating spirit taking advantage of my mistakes, loose your hold over my life.
15. Every spirit manipulating me to disobey the law of God, you will not prosper over my life
16. Every spirit manipulating me to eat the forbidden fruit, you will not prosper over my life.
17. Every spirit manipulating me to work against myself, you will not prosper over my life.
18. Every spirit manipulating me in order to rob me of my glory, you will not prosper over my life.
19. Every spirit manipulating me in order to rob me of my joy, you will not prosper over my life.
20. Every spirit manipulating me in order to rob me of my miracles, you will not prosper over my life.

21. Every spirit manipulating me in order to rob me of my blessing, you will not prosper over my life.
22. Every spirit manipulating me in order to rob me of my breakthroughs, you will not prosper over my life.
23. Every spirit manipulating me in order to rob me of my success, you will not prosper over my life.
24. Every spirit manipulating me in order to rob me of my promotion, you will not prosper over my life.
25. Every spirit manipulating me in order to neutralize the power of God in me, you will not prosper over my life.
26. Every spirit manipulating me in order to corrupt my anointing, you will not prosper over my life.
27. Every spirit manipulating me to work against my own destiny, you will not prosper over my life.
28. Every spirit manipulating me to work against God's plan for my life, you will not prosper over my life.
29. Every spirit manipulating me to move out of my appointed location, you will not prosper over me.
30. Every spirit manipulating me in order to miss my open heaven, you will not prosper over my life.

I cover my prayers in the blood of Jesus Christ. According to the Word of God, I have asked, I shall receive. I have knocked the door, it shall be opened unto me. I have sought, I shall find, in the name of Jesus Christ. It is written, "… Decree a thing, and it shall be established". As I have spoken in prayer, it shall be so. My prayers shall produce desire results. My prayers shall produce desired miracles. My prayers shall produce desired testimonies, in the name of Jesus Christ. Territorial spirit and power cannot hinder this prayer. Sins and flesh cannot hinder this prayer. It is done. It is sealed by the blood of Jesus Christ. It is delivered to me, in Jesus might name. Amen!

DAY FOURTEEN

PRAYER FOR A DRAMATIC CHANGE

Passages To Read Before You Pray:
John 9:1-25, Joel 2:21-27, 1 Samuel 30:1-25, Psalms 42, 86, 30

In the book of Job 22:28, the Scripture says when I decree a thing, it shall be established for me. I stand on this Scripture and decree. I have come into the presence of God today to plead my case. I enter through the gate of praise into the sanctuary of heaven. I cover myself in the precious blood of Jesus Christ. I baptize myself in the fire of the Holy Ghost. I charge this atmosphere with the fire of God, and I take this neighborhood for the Lord. I arrest every principality and power, territorial spirit, and every throne and kingdom that is not of God. I cast you down and I command you never to lift yourself up against me, because I have the life of God in me.

In the name of Jesus Christ, I confess my sins today, and I ask you O Lord to forgive me on the basis of your mercy. With all my heart, I forgive those who have sinned against me from the past through this moment. I release them from any form of guilt and shame, in the name of Jesus Christ. I hereby plead the blood of Jesus over any sins committed by my parents and ancestors. I cancel through the Blood of Jesus Christ, any satanic covenants, exchanges, vows or transactions made over my life, body, soul, spirit, and circumstances, in the name of Jesus Christ. I cancel every legal right that the devil may have against me, by the blood of Jesus Christ. The accuser of the brethren will have nothing against me as I come to the presence of God in prayer.

The devil cannot hinder or delay my prayer, because I know who I am. I am a child of the Kingdom; I am a king and priest of the

Lord, redeemed from the hand of the devil by the blood of Jesus Christ. I declare that all satanic thrones, altars, dominions, principalities, powers, rulers of darkness, queen of the coast, queen of heavens, household wickedness, spiritual hosts of wickedness and all satanic works, have no power or authority over my life. I declare that satanic harassment and intimidation have no effect on me.

Today I receive divine strength to pray; I will not pray in vain. I will not pray amiss. My prayers will bring the desired results. I command the fountain of prayer to open now, and flow into my life, I command the warring angels of God to descend and fight on my behalf. Every minute and every hour that I spend in prayer will bring solution. Every prayer point will attract divine attention and divine intervention. I decree open heavens over my prayers, and today, God of heaven and earth will attend to my case. My prayers today will shake the heavens and move the earth; testimonies, miracles, healing, breakthrough, signs and wonders will follow my prayers. At the end of this prayer session, my life will never be the same again.

PRAYER POINTS

1. O God my Father, thank you for being my God, my Father and my friend.
2. O God my Father, thank you for the privilege to know you and the power of the resurrection of Jesus Christ.
3. O God my Father, thank you for always being there for me and with me.
4. O God my Father, thank y/ou for the great and mighty things that you are doing in my life.

5. O God my Father, thank you for your provision and protection over me and my household.
6. O God my Father, thank you for always answering my prayers.
7. I confess my sins before you today and I ask you to forgive me on the basis of your mercy, in the name of Jesus Christ.
8. Wash me clean today O Lord by the blood of Jesus Christ.
9. I cover myself and my household with the blood of Jesus Christ.
10. My prayers today will not go in vain; my prayers will produce the desired results in the name of Jesus Christ.
11. O God my Father, arise today, touch me and change my story for the best, in the name of Jesus Christ.
12. O God my Father, arise today, touch me and change my situation for the best, in the name of Jesus Christ.
13. O God my Father, arise today, touch me and change the circumstances around me for the best, in the name of Jesus Christ.
14. Arise today O Lord, and restore my life back to your original plan, in the name of Jesus Christ.
15. O God my Father, let all my wasted efforts be restored unto me this month, in the name of Jesus Christ.
16. O God my Father, let everything that the enemy has destroyed in my life be restored unto me now, in the name of Jesus Christ.
17. O God arise and restore unto me the years that demonic locusts have eaten in my life, in the name of Jesus Christ.

18. O God arise and restore unto me all my efforts that demonic locusts have wasted, in the name of Jesus Christ.
19. O God arise and restore unto me everything that demonic locusts have destroyed in my life, in the name of Jesus Christ.
20. O God arise and restore unto me my finances that demonic locusts have devoured, in the name of Jesus Christ.
21. O God arise and restore unto me every good thing in my life that demonic locusts have eaten, in the name of Jesus Christ.
22. I release the fire of God to destroy demonic locusts eating away my joy, in the name of Jesus Christ.
23. I release the fire of God to destroy demonic locusts eating away my success, in the name of Jesus Christ.
24. I release the fire of God to destroy demonic locusts eating away my peace, in the name of Jesus Christ.
25. I release the fire of God to destroy demonic locusts devouring my finances, in the name of Jesus Christ.
26. I release the fire of God to destroy demonic locusts sent to destroy the works of my hands, in the name of Jesus Christ.
27. I release the fire of God to destroy demonic locusts sent to destroy my harvests, in the name of Jesus Christ.
28. I release the fire of God to destroy demonic locusts sent to stop my breakthroughs, in the name of Jesus Christ.
29. O God my Father, arise and restore unto me everything that demonic cankerworms have destroyed in my life, in the name of Jesus Christ.

30. O God my Father, arise and restore unto me the years of my life that demonic cankerworms have eaten, in the name of Jesus Christ.
31. O God my Father, arise and restore unto me the years of my life that demonic cankerworms have wasted, in the name of Jesus Christ.
32. O God my Father, arise and restore unto me all good things in my life that demonic cankerworms have eaten, in the name of Jesus Christ.
33. O God my Father, arise and restore unto me today all my harvests that demonic cankerworms have eaten, in the name of Jesus Christ.
34. O God my Father, arise and restore unto me today, all my miracles that demonic cankerworms have eaten, in the name of Jesus Christ.
35. O God my Father, arise and restore unto me all my blessings that demonic cankerworms have eaten, in the name of Jesus Christ.
36. O God my Father, arise and restore unto me the joy of my marriage that demonic cankerworms have eaten, in the name of Jesus Christ.
37. O God my Father, arise and restore unto me the joy over my children that demonic cankerworms have eaten, in the name of Jesus Christ.
38. O God my Father, arise and restore unto me the works of my hands that demonic cankerworms have destroyed, in the name of Jesus Christ.
39. O God my Father, arise and restore unto me the fulfillment of promises that demonic cankerworms have taken away from me, in the name of Jesus Christ.

40. O God my Father, arise and restore unto me my breakthroughs that demonic cankerworms have stopped, in the name of Jesus Christ.
41. I release the fire of God to destroy every demonic cankerworm sent to destroy me, in the name of Jesus Christ.
42. I release the fire of God to destroy every demonic cankerworm sent to destroy the works of my hands, in the name of Jesus Christ.
43. I release the fire of God to destroy every demonic cankerworm eating away my joy, in the name of Jesus Christ.
44. I release the fire of God to destroy every demonic cankerworm eating away my miracles, in the name of Jesus Christ.
45. I release the fire of God to destroy every demonic cankerworm devouring my finances, in the name of Jesus Christ.
46. I release the fire of God to destroy every demonic cankerworm sent to waste my good efforts, in the name of Jesus Christ.
47. I release the fire of God to destroy every demonic cankerworm sent to attack my marriage, in the name of Jesus Christ.
48. I release the fire of God to destroy every demonic cankerworm sent to attack my health, in the name of Jesus Christ.
49. I release the fire of God to destroy every demonic cankerworm sent to attack my family, in the name of Jesus Christ.

50. I release the fire of God to destroy every demonic cankerworm sent to attack my spouse, in the name of Jesus Christ.
51. I release the fire of God to destroy every demonic cankerworm sent to attack my children, in the name of Jesus Christ.
52. I release the fire of God to destroy every demonic cankerworm sent to attack my spiritual life, in the name of Jesus Christ.
53. I release the fire of God to destroy every demonic cankerworm sent to attack my prayer life, in the name of Jesus Christ.
54. I release the fire of God to destroy every demonic cankerworm sent to attack my prayer altar, in the name of Jesus Christ.
55. I release the fire of God to destroy every demonic cankerworm eating away my ability to produce success, in the name of Jesus Christ.
56. I release the fire of God to destroy every demonic cankerworm eating away my ability to fulfill purpose, in the name of Jesus Christ.
57. I release the fire of God to destroy every demonic cankerworm eating away my ability to fulfill destiny, in the name of Jesus Christ.

I cover my prayers in the blood of Jesus Christ. According to the Word of God, I have asked, I shall receive. I have knocked the door, it shall be opened unto me. I have sought, I shall find, in the name of Jesus Christ. It is written, "... Decree a thing, and it shall be established". As I have spoken in prayer, it shall be so. My prayers shall produce desire results. My prayers shall produce desired miracles. My prayers shall produce desired testimonies, in the name of Jesus Christ. Territorial spirit and power cannot hinder this prayer. Sins and flesh cannot hinder this prayer. It is done. It is sealed by the blood of Jesus Christ. It is delivered to me, in Jesus might name. Amen!

Books by Timothy Atunnise

I Must Win This Battle

I Must Win This Battle offers a hands-on training self-deliverance process and prayers. It covers over 2000 prayer points focusing on how to remove unwanted and unwanted situations of life. Battle of life is a must win for every child of God and this book shows how to, in a very simple and effective way. It is a must have for every household.

Let There Be A Change

"Let There Be A Change" is a must have Personal Deliverance prayer book that will transform your life and bring restoration into every area of your life. What is Deliverance? Deliverance means to loose the bounds of wickedness. A lot of people are under the bondage of wickedness. If you look at the lives of many people, you will discover a wide array of wicked occurrences. If your life is surrounded by wicked mysterious happenings, you need to seek deliverance as soon as possible. Deliverance centers on the destruction of the yoke of the enemy. A yoke is anything that hinders or sets you back. Whatever sets you back from moving forward in your life is a yoke. God's will is that you move forward and attain divine goals set for your life. When the contrary happens, there is a bondage hanging above your life. Deliverance is to break curses and evil covenants. The ancestors of many people were cursed and the curses have flown down the family line. For example, if a person struggles without any tangible achievement in life, there is a problem somewhere.

Earth Moving Prayers

"I have seen the affliction of my people, and have heard their cry by reason of their enemies and tormentors, for I know their sorrows; and I have come down to deliver them out of the hand of the wicked and unrepentant enemies. And I will surely bring to pass my plans and counsels concerning them." This is the Word of the Lord that gave birth to this Anointed Prayer Book, "EARTH-MOVING PRAYERS". Earth-Moving Prayers is a highly anointed deliverance prayer book that will transform your life, and set you free from any form of bondage or captivity you may find yourself. Over 600 pages of mountain moving and yoke destroying prayer points. Over 5300 problems solving and solution finding prayer points prepared by the Holy Ghost to set you free. If you are ready to take your life back from that terrible situation, this book is for you, a must have for every household.

Total Deliverance – Volume 1

"Why would you pay for a debt that you did not owe? Why would you have to be what the enemies want your life to be? The plan of God for you is to live freely and prosper as He has promised in the Scriptures. You do not have to pay for the sins of your parents or ancestors; you don't have to go through what they went through, your life is different and your case is different. If you can just believe, the Bible says, "You will see the glory of God." – John 11:40.

This book is loaded with prayers that will transform your life, deliver you from ancestral curses, generational and foundational curses, self-inflicted curses, break yokes and destroy bondages no matter how long it's been there."

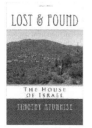

Lost & Found: The House of Israel

Lost & Found "The House of Israel" offers detailed information about the past, present and future of the House of Israel. Jacob released special blessings upon two of his children, he gave Joseph the Birthright and Judah the Kingdom. God made covenant with David that he will always have a son on his throne and his throne will be everlasting. In this book, you will discover where the throne of David is currently and how it got there. It is a must for every Bible student.

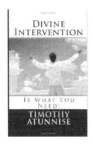

Divine Intervention

Deliverance centers on the destruction of the yoke of the enemy. A yoke is anything that hinders or sets you back. Whatever sets you back from moving forward in your life is a yoke.

God's will is that you move forward and attain divine goals set for your life. When the contrary happens, there is a bondage hanging above your life.

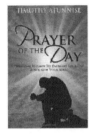

Prayer of The Day – Volume 1

How wonderful would it be to start your day with joy and end it with great success? The Spirit of the Lord led me to write Prayer of the Day, a wonderful, daily spiritual vitamin. He promised that this book would touch and change many lives and situations for the better as people began to commit every day to the hands of God, for He knows the beginning and ending. Prayer is communion with God. Through prayer we actually experience relationship with God. The quality of our prayer life determines the quality of our relationship with God. I promise you, in the name of the Lord, that you will experience the power of God, great deliverance and a move of the Holy Spirit in your life as you join millions of people across the globe in prayer every morning before you start your day.

Prayer of The Day – Volume 2

How wonderful would it be to start your day with joy and end it with great success? The Spirit of the Lord led me to write Prayer of the Day, a wonderful, daily spiritual vitamin. He promised that this book would touch and change many lives and situations for the better as people began to commit every day to the hands of God, for He knows the beginning and ending. Prayer is communion with God. Through prayer we actually experience relationship with God. The quality of our prayer life determines the quality of our relationship with God. I promise you, in the name of the Lord, that you will experience the power of God, great deliverance and a move of the Holy Spirit in your life as you join millions of people across the globe in prayer every morning before you start your day.

Overcoming Self

Sunday School manual

The King Is Coming

The King Is Coming teaches the End-Times messages and prophecies. It is very accurate and easy to understand. It shows the application of the Word of God to current affairs, and establishing the truth of what is happening in world today in the Scripture. It is written to prepare the Saints for that Glorious Hope and for the End-Times assignments (End-Times Revival).

The Fruit of The Spirit

Fruit of the Spirit is mentioned in several areas of the Bible. However, the most applicable passage is Galatians 5:22-23 where Paul actually lists out the fruits. Paul used this list to show the contrast between a Godly character and one that is focused on fleshly concerns. These are not just individual "fruits" (attributes) from which to pick and choose. Rather, the fruit of the Spirit is one ninefold "fruit" that characterizes all who truly walk in the Holy Spirit. In order to understand the fruit of the Spirit, we must first understand who the Spirit is, what He does and how He helps us live our lives pleasing to God. The questions are: What are the Fruits of the Spirit? How can you develop them? What does that mean for you? What fruits of the Spirit do you have?

The Parables of Jesus Christ

A parable is a story in which a real and earthly thing is used to parallel or illustrate a spiritual or heavenly thing. Such a story acts as a "riddle" that both veils and reveals all at once -- veiling the spiritual behind words that reveal the earthly and which can be penetrated to reach the spiritual by those "who have ears to hear." Jesus tells us that He spoke in parables precisely to veil and reveal, to speak, in a sense, "secretly" while not in secret at all.

The Miracles of Jesus Christ

Understanding the story of the healing and miracles of Jesus Christ. Christ came into the world, not only as God's personal representative on earth, but as God manifest in flesh. He was Himself a miracle in human form, and His miraculous works are bound up inseparably with His life. "The blind receive their sight and the lame walk; the lepers are cleansed and the deaf hear; the dead are raised up and the poor have the gospel preached to them". His miracles provided proof of who He was.

Bible Study: The Book of Exodus

This Bible study is designed as an expository study of the Book of Exodus, taking the student through large portions of this Old Testament book with cross references to other portions of Scripture. The purpose is to assist the student in gaining a greater comprehension of the biblical teaching contained in the Book of Exodus with an emphasis on practical application. This study presents introductory information about the Book of Exodus followed by twenty-two lessons devoted to an in-depth study of the biblical text. The student will begin by exploring a portion of Exodus with the help of a series of exploratory questions. There will then follow an in-depth study of the passage, guided by an expositional commentary on the text. The student should prepare for his study by asking the Holy Spirit to enlighten his mind and open his heart to receive not only the teaching of Scripture but Christ Himself as He is presented in the Scriptures.

Essential Prayers:
(Prayers That Bring Total Victory)

Essential Prayers is an anointed prayer book that touches every aspect of life. It offers ways to make prayers more personal and powerful, and how to establish a practice of prayer that works. Essential Prayers is for every Christian home, it will surely transform your prayer life and reshape your entire outlook of life.

Essential Prayers addresses your personal situations, it provides prayers for marriage restoration, total victory, financial release, deliverance from addiction, prayer against problems started in childhood, foundational problems, prayer for singles, prayer against ancestral debt-collectors, prayer for signs and wonders, and many more.

We are given the authority and power to take over, not to be run over. If you fail to take over, you'll be run over. Essential Prayers offers step-by-step prayer guidelines to take over and possess your possessions.

PRAYER CDs by TIMOTHY ATUNNISE

1. Pray Before You Start Your Day
2. Pray Before You Go To Bed
3. Overcoming Impossibilities
4. Prayer To Overcome Poverty
5. Prayer To Break Evil Cycles
6. Prayer To Stop Demonic Activities
7. Prayer For Business Prosperity
8. Secret of Finding God's Rest
9. Spiritual House Cleansing
10. Take Your Life Back By Force
11. Prayer To Overcome Limitations
12. Prayer To Cancel Untimely Death
13. Prayer To Break Curses of Poverty & Empty Pocket
14. Prayer For Victory Over Bad Dreams
15. Prayer For Uncommon Favor
16. Prayer For Supernatural Breakthroughs
17. Prayer To Break Ungodly Soul-Ties
18. Prayer To Overcome Financial Setbacks
19. Prayer To Destroy The Works of The Devil
20. Prayer To Overturn Stubborn Situations
21. Prayer To Close Evil Chapters
22. Prayer For Instant Miracles
23. Shaping Your Children's Future
24. Prayer For Restoration
25. I Must Win This Battle
26. The Secret of Knowing God

DELIVERANCE PRAYER CDs by TIMOTHY ATUNNISE

1. Prayer For Self-Deliverance
2. Healing The Wounded Heart
3. Prevention & Deliverance From Cancer
4. Deliverance From Evil Covenant
5. Deliverance From The Devourer
6. Deliverance & Healing Prayer
7. Identify Your Spiritual Territory (Parts 1 & 2)
8. Exercise Spiritual Authority
9. Casting Out Spirits   (Parts 1 & 2)
10. Curses & How To Deal With Them   (Parts 1 & 2)
11. How Demons Enter & Oppress People (Parts 1 & 2)
12. Deliverance From Jezebel's Spirit
13. Defeating The Strongman
14. Deliverance From The Terrible
15. Deliverance From Curses of Last-Minute Failure
16. Deliverance From Curses of Rejection

WORSHIP CDs

1. Christocentric – Worship Songs
2. I Am That I Am
3. Yahweh Reigns

Note

Note

Read
Deut 2:7
Deut 8:17 — Repeat daily
Deut 30:9 For Prosperity (Money)
I Chron 29:12 Release
Psalm 18:20, 21
Ps 144:1
Prov 12:24
Ecc 11:6